IT'S THE
THOUGHT
THAT
COUNTS

IT'S THE THOUGHT THAT COUNTS

The Astounding Evidence
for the Power of Mind
over Matter

David R. Hamilton, PhD

HAY HOUSE

Australia • Canada • Hong Kong
South Africa • United Kingdom • United States

First published and distributed in the United Kingdom by:
Hay House UK Ltd, 292B Kensal Rd, London W10 5BE.
Tel.: (44) 20 8962 1230; Fax: (44) 20 8962 1239. www.hayhouse.co.uk

Published and distributed in the United States of America by:
Hay House, Inc., PO Box 5100, Carlsbad, CA 92018-5100.
Tel.: (1) 760 431 7695 or (800) 654 5126; Fax: (1) 760 431 6948 or (800) 650 5115.
www.hayhouse.com

Published and distributed in Australia by:
Hay House Australia Ltd, 18/36 Ralph St, Alexandria NSW 2015.
Tel.: (61) 2 9669 4299; Fax: (61) 2 9669 4144. www.hayhouse.com.au

Published and distributed in the Republic of South Africa by:
Hay House SA (Pty), Ltd, PO Box 990, Witkoppen 2068.
Tel./Fax: (27) 11 706 6612. orders@psdprom.co.za

Distributed in Canada by:
Raincoast, 9050 Shaughnessy St, Vancouver, BC V6P 6E5.
Tel.: (1) 604 323 7100; Fax: (1) 604 323 2600

The author of this book does not dispense medical advice or prescribe the use of any
technique as a form of treatment for physical or medical problems without the advice
of a physician, either directly or indirectly. The intent of the author is only to offer
information of a general nature to help you in your quest for emotional and spiritual
well-being. In the event you use any of the information in this book for yourself, which
is your constitutional right, the author and the publisher assume no responsibility
for your actions.

A catalogue record for this book is available from the British Library.

This title was previously self-published by the author.

ISBN 1-4019-1168-4
ISBN 978-1-4019-1168-3

Printed and bound in Europe for Imago.

For Elizabeth...

CONTENTS

FOREWORD

I'm grateful to David Hamilton for writing this inspiring book. As a scientist who has embraced new consciousness, he has made a bridge that will be helpful to many people who are seeking to understand the connection between our body, our mind and our spiritual self. David has lovingly collected together research from scientists, healers and mystics to provide people with a rational and scientific explanation of the true nature of our universe.

I am sure David's insights will help to increase people's understanding and conviction that we are composed of energy. Integrating this truth into our lives will empower people to live every day in the conscious understanding that every thought directly affects and shapes our world.

David's aim in writing this book is to inspire people to live a love-filled life. It would be hard to read his ideas and not become a more consciously loving human.

Louise L. Hay
August 2006

ACKNOWLEDGEMENTS

I consider myself to be blessed in being surrounded by so many kind, patient, understanding and generous people, and would like to thank a few of them here.

I would like to thank my life partner Elizabeth Caproni. Her never-ending love and support have been an inspiration to me and have often lifted me and guided me along my current path. Without her, this book would never have gained its present form.

I would also like to thank my parents, Janette and Robert Hamilton, who brought me into this world, loved me and supported me throughout every endeavour of my life, and who taught me from an early age that 'It's the thought that counts.'

I would also like to thank Elma and Peter Caproni, who made me a part of their family and loved me and supported me through numerous challenging times.

I am also grateful for the many friends, past and present, who helped guide me on my spiritual path. In particular I will always remember the journey of Spirit Aid and all who participated in it.

For doing an excellent job of editing this book, I would like to thank Lizzie Hutchins. I am also very grateful to Michelle Pilley at Hay House UK for making me feel so welcome in the Hay House family.

A great big thank you to all who patiently read this book and offered me feedback: Margaret McCathie, Kenny McCathie, June Moore, Siobhan Moore, Ann Brocklebank, Stan Giles, Liz Ivory, Bryce Redford, Joyce Bunton, Dave Clarkson, Olivia Barham, Kenny McDougall, Seth Gardiner and Andrea Lomas. I would also like to thank Thom Hartmann and Louise Hay for endorsing the book.

For helpful answers to some of my questions regarding Chapter 3, I would like to thank Professor Eric Kandel, year 2000 Nobel Laureate in Medicine. I would also like to thank Dr Ernest Rossi for helpful answers and for taking the time to send me some important scientific publications on psychosocial genomics that helped Chapter 3 develop into its present form. This help was given having never seen the book.

I would also like to thank Glasgow University, the Homoeopathic Hospital in Glasgow and Paul Stevens in the Koestler Parapsychology Unit of Edinburgh University for helping me to obtain valuable scientific information for the book.

To all the scientists who have painstakingly carried out the research that I have reported in this book, you have helped many people to recognize that what they always thought might be true really is.

INTRODUCTION

This book describes how our thoughts and feelings, ideas and beliefs and hopes and dreams alter the condition of our bodies, the circumstances of our lives and even the state of the world.

Every thought counts!

The latest scientific discoveries are revealing that every thought and feeling we ever have is expressed throughout our bodies. For instance, the way we appreciate someone in our life or think about someone whose actions stress us causes changes in our bodies.

Molecules known as neuropeptides link our thoughts and emotions to every part of our bodies. This is why placebos heal people in medical trials. If a person believes they are receiving real medicine, or even if they simply believe in the doctor who administers it, they will usually get better.

Our thoughts and feelings even switch genes on and off. Scientific studies have recently shown that they can cause new areas of growth in our brains, which eventually leads to changes in our bodies. In a very real sense, you are what you think!

The mind-body link even opens up the opportunity for us to heal ourselves of illnesses through the power of our intentions. Stress, for instance, slows down the rate of repair from illness. But if you choose to focus on something that pleases you or think kind thoughts about a person you care about, your body will produce many fewer stress hormones and so the healing process will speed up.

Scientific studies have even indicated that placing your hands upon a person can affect the conditions in *their* body. Studies on rat pups, for instance, have shown that a mother's touch increases levels of growth hormones and reduces stress hormones.

Even visualizing a person in good health helps. You don't need to be near them for this to work either. Quantum scientists have shown that everything in existence is connected. A thought about anything, wherever it is, changes it in some way.

A thought about a person, then, is registered at some level in their body. Scientists have studied this and found nervous system changes in test subjects as a result of the thoughts that other people are holding about them.

But a thought about *anything* has the same type of effect, even though we don't always notice it. Researchers have studied this and noticed particularly large effects when many people are focusing on the same thing at the same time. Such group intentions have been shown to reduce crime rates and even instances of terrorism.

Such is our connection to everything that it is impossible for us *not* to affect the state of the world by what we choose to focus on. An attitude of kindness or forgiveness, for instance, will lead to different conditions – in your body, your life and in the world – than an attitude of selfishness or vengeance. It sounds like common sense – but this book explains *how* it works and, importantly, what you can do to change things for the better.

Much of the science in this book has already been published in peer-reviewed scientific journals, the gold standard in science. I have merely extracted the relevant portions and made a few extrapolations from the conclusions of some of the research, fusing them with my own ideas, which have derived from a broad view of the fields of mind-body science, spirituality and consciousness.

Some of the science presented here has not met with such peer-reviewed approval yet, although this doesn't mean that it is invalid. New ideas and discoveries often take time before they break through into what is regarded as the mainstream. I do believe that many of the studies mentioned in this book point towards a real phenomenon. I believe that we are on the brink of a major breakthrough in our understanding of consciousness and the interplay between mind and matter.

Some of the research I present might sound 'way out there', especially to the average academic scientist. I make no apologies for this. As history has shown us, the path of scientific discovery frequently leads to what at first appears to be ridiculous and it is only later that our understanding of the way things work enables us to embrace the new ideas.

The second half of the book brings spirituality into play. There is less science in this part and more use of intuition as I present a mystical view of the world that is probably beyond scientific proof and can only be grasped by personal experience. But this is still science, only a different kind of science, one that is peculiar to the individual, making everyone a scientist in their own life.

I end the book in the way I like to end all of my talks – helping people to recognize the love, kindness and compassion everywhere around them. When we choose to love, to be kind and to exercise compassion in our personal lives, everything changes. Everything. Go on, try it out! Let us begin our journey of change.

David R. Hamilton, PhD
May 2006

1
Body and Mind

Body and mind are intertwined. Every thought, feeling and intention you have sends ripples throughout your body. The results depend upon the nature of those thoughts, feelings and intentions. They can be so powerful that they even affect your genes. A particular gene that might produce a disease or protect you from disease, for example, can be switched on and off according to how you process the daily experiences of your life. The implications of this are enormous. Every function of the human body is susceptible to thoughts and feelings.

The entire body is actually hardwired to feel every emotion. And as it does so, our emotional challenges frequently show up as physical symptoms. Although there are many different causes of cancer, for instance, one factor that seems to have an influence is the suppression of negative emotion. It has been shown that cancer generally progresses fastest in people who hold in deep emotional pain which has often built up over many years. The great news is that releasing the pain can halt and even reverse the cancer.

We regularly cure aches, pains, illnesses and diseases using our minds, although most of the time we are unaware of doing so. Science has proven that a person who believes they are receiving medicine, even though it is really a dummy – a placebo – will usually be cured. In one scientific study, patients were given morphine for serious pain every day for three days, but on the fourth day the morphine was secretly swapped for a placebo – a saltwater solution. Yet the patients experienced pain relief as they had before and medical tests even recorded the same physiological changes as when they had received morphine. Their belief alone had neutralized the pain.

Placebo effects like these rely on blind faith, but everyone can learn to harness the power of their thoughts and feelings to bring about positive health effects in their own body. Visualization techniques, for instance, are regularly used by thousands of people and have often produced what may be seen as nothing short of miracles.

We can even heal each other. Numerous methods of healing by touch are used by a growing number of people all over the world. In fact, a 1998 study estimated that over 40,000 nurses in the USA practised such therapies. That number is much greater now. In the UK, a year 2000 estimate suggested that there were around three times more practitioners of Reiki than there were doctors and nurses.

There is a large volume of research to back up these therapies, much of it conducted under strict scientifically controlled conditions. Some of these studies even show that people can mentally influence the growth rate of biological organisms held in test tubes. Amazing but true!

Studies have also shown why it is that many people are aware of when someone is staring at them. Researchers found that people sitting in one room were responding to thoughts people in another room 25 metres away were having about them. While they were hooked up to scientific instruments, their skin showed minor changes in electrical resistance depending upon the type of thought the other people were having about them.

All of these studies, and many more, will be discussed later in the book. So too will be the fact that according to our thoughts, feelings and beliefs, we create the experiences of our lives. The good news is that we can change aspects of our lives simply by changing our attitudes.

Collectively, we also create events in the world. As well as showing that the body and mind are connected, science has also demonstrated that we are intimately connected to each other in such a way that every thought and feeling sends ripples throughout the entire universe.

While each person has what may be called a 'mental and emotional climate' representing their general mental and emotional state, we all share a collective mental and emotional climate. And just as our personal climates influence what happens to us in our personal lives, so our collective climate influences what happens to us on a world scale. What goes on all over the world is merely a projection of how we, collectively, think and feel.

But before we get ahead of ourselves, let us first explore some of the obvious ways in which the body and mind are connected.

The Bodymind

Have you ever realized that when you cry it is your thoughts and feelings that cause your body to produce tears? Thoughts and feelings of happiness or sadness set in motion a series of internal events in your body that climax in a deluge of tears. Mind affecting biology! Similarly, an embarrassing thought might turn your face red. A pleasant thought, on the other hand, can alter the rhythms of your heart and even raise the strength of your immune system.

Sexual arousal is also a mind-body phenomenon. Imagination alone can cause hormonal changes in women and obvious physical changes in men. In these very common ways, thoughts and emotions influence your biology.

On the health front you are probably well aware that stressful thinking can cause a whole range of illnesses, and this has been well documented in the scientific literature. Have you ever imagined the dire consequences of not getting something done on time or stressed yourself out at the thought of being late for an appointment? That sort of stress can eventually bring about the internal bodily changes that lead to heart disease. But ultimately, the events did not cause the disease, the mental processes did. It wasn't being late – it was your thoughts *about* being late.

The health effects of how we think and feel are extremely far-reaching. Most medical professionals will agree that the state of mind of many patients admitted to their surgeries is indeed responsible for their illness.

What is less well known, but also true, is the reverse: that your biology can affect your thoughts and emotions. This is pretty obvious if you think about it. For example, when a woman has her period there are hormonal changes in her body that cause emotional ups and downs which affect her thinking. Changes in her biology therefore bring about changes in her thoughts and emotions.

Furthermore, chemical changes in the brain can make a person feel emotionally high or low. For example, opiate drugs like heroin and morphine can alter emotions. Endorphins, which are the body's own natural opiates, do a similar job.

So mind-body communication goes both ways – mind to body and body to mind – and it is so smooth that many scientists now refer to the body and mind as the same thing – the 'bodymind' – just as they refer to space and time as 'space-time'. One cannot be disentangled from the other.

A lot of modern research has been done into this. For instance, the Institute of Heartmath published a scientific study in 1995 in the *American Journal of Cardiology* which showed the effects of some forms of positive or negative thinking on the heart. They found that thoughts of appreciation and anger produced opposite effects in the body.

In the study, 12 people were asked to think 'appreciation' and another 12 were asked to think 'anger'. Meanwhile scientists monitored their hearts. After performing computer analysis on the heartbeats, the scientists discovered that the hearts of the people thinking 'appreciation' had been beating more smoothly and regularly   called 'internal coherence' – than the hearts of the people who were thinking 'anger'. And this type of coherence has a knock-on effect on the rest of your body.

It is well known that something that is vibrating coherently can 'entrain' neighbouring objects to the same smooth rhythm. For example, if you were to swing a large pendulum and lots of smaller pendulums at different rates in a room, then leave and come back later, the smaller pendulums would be swinging to the same rhythm as the large one. The large pendulum would have entrained, or 'inspired', the smaller pendulums.

Similarly, if you hit a tuning fork it will inspire nearby tuning forks to vibrate at the same speed.

Internal coherence in the heart entrains other organs into a similar coherent and healthy state. In a sense, positive thinking can cause all of the organs to sing to the same tune, bringing balance and harmony to the body. You have probably noticed in your personal life that when you feel consistently positive, people sing to the same tune as you and your whole life develops a degree of balance and harmony. The same thing happens in your body.

In another study the Institute of Heartmath also showed that positive and negative thinking could affect the body's immune system. Researchers monitored the amounts of salivary immunoglobulin A (s-IgA) after each person in the study thought 'care and compassion' or 'anger and frustration'. Salivary immunoglobulin A is a part of the immune system found in the saliva that can neutralize the bacteria that enter your mouth, from your food for example. A large amount of it indicates a strong immune system, whereas a small amount indicates a weakened system.

The Heartmath scientists found that 'care and compassion' produced a stronger immune system than 'anger and frustration'. In fact, they found that just five minutes of 'care and compassion' caused the immune system to be elevated for five hours, while five minutes of 'anger and frustration' depressed it for five hours. So, we can create positive states of health by thinking positive.

In 2005, a scientific study showed just this. When shown pictures that would usually bring about a negative emotion – for instance, a picture of a burns victim – test subjects were taught to change the meaning of the picture in their minds.

So, for this type of picture they might 'reappraise' it as, perhaps, a picture of an actor wearing make-up to film a scene for a movie. As they did this, their level of negative emotion reduced significantly. Using fMRI brain scans, the study even showed real changes in their brains as they reinterpreted the picture. And due to the link between mind and body, these changes would be expressed throughout the body.

In everyday life, we often interpret things that we see and experiences that we have, based on assumptions. But often these assumptions are just that – no more. We do not know the real truth. But when they are negative, these assumptions do bring about real negative states in our minds and bodies.

Some people use daily affirmations to keep their minds positive. For example, a well-known affirmation created by French psychotherapist Emile Coué reads: 'Every day in every way I am getting better and better.' Studies have revealed that such positive affirmations are enough to strengthen the immune system.

Another route to generating a positive attitude is laughter, which is also mind-body communication. When you hear a funny joke or see something funny it is the mental associations you make that produce the laughter, causing your 'side-splitting' movements. The physical shaking, coupled with the huge grin on your face, is the last thing to happen. A lot more goes on beneath the surface, all initiated by your mental pictures. For instance, laughter increases oxygen levels in the blood. It also produces endorphins (feel-good hormones), which explains why it makes you feel so good. It also affects the entire hormone (endocrine) system. Scientific studies have even shown that it strengthens the immune system and therefore helps the body to keep disease away.

If you are remembering a time when you laughed heartily then your body will probably be undergoing these kinds of changes right now. You might even be able to feel them.

Meditation

So we know that looking at life light-heartedly and positively can create good health, but it is not always easy to be consistently positive. With the exception of Homer Simpson and a few meditation masters, most people's minds are chaotic, constantly jumping back and forth between topics and initiating a range of moods. And the body mirrors the mind – a chaotic mind inspires chaotic biology.

Changing this is one of the goals of meditation. During meditation, as the mind becomes peaceful, the body's functions become more coherent and so the body becomes healthier. Consistent meditation helps retain this state in daily life.

A 2006 report described a study where children with ADHD were taught meditation (a form known as Transcendental Meditation). The scientists found that through the practice of sitting with their eyes closed and focusing on a particular word for 10 minutes twice a day, the children experienced about a 50 per cent reduction in stress, anxiety and depression, and many of them reported that they consistently felt calmer.

Meditation has been the subject of a great deal of scientific study, particularly since the arrival of Indian yogi Paramahansa Yogananda in the USA in 1920. He described spiritual masters, whom he called 'saints', who lived to great ages, rarely contracted illnesses and could perform great feats. Among other things they practised kriya yoga, which is a form of meditation based upon scientific principles.

Since that time several hundred scientific studies have been conducted on meditation and how it affects health. Some of them have pointed to why these saints could defy the normal ageing process.

One of the main reasons our bodies wear out as we age is because of a gradual deterioration of the endocrine system, which is the hormonal engine in the body. A drop in the levels of some important hormones accompanies this deterioration. For instance, levels of human growth hormone, which helps to keep us healthy and repair our bodies, and the hormone DHEA (dehydroepiandrosterone), which helps to minimize stress, improve memory and protect the brain from damage, usually drop as we age.

One of the main factors affecting the deterioration of the endocrine system is the wear and tear brought about by mental and emotional stress. So stress speeds up ageing. You have probably heard stories of people under extreme stress whose hair turned white almost overnight.

Meditation is often used as an antidote to stress and has been found to increase DHEA levels. In fact, in a meditation study a group of 45-year-old males who regularly meditated were found to have 23 per cent more DHEA than a similar group who didn't meditate. In women, the meditators had 47 per cent more DHEA.

Another scientific study found that for every 20 per cent increase in DHEA there was a 48 per cent drop in heart disease and a 36 per cent drop in death from any cause.

A study into Transcendental Meditation even found that people who practised it for more than five years were physiologically 12 years younger than their chronological age. Could it be that meditation is better than Botox?

Some forms of meditation use visualization, although visualization alone can have an effect on health. In the book *Creating Miracles* by Carolyn Miller, MD, there is a story of a man who used a visualization technique that he learned from Shakti Gawain's bestselling book *Creative Visualization*. Once fit and active, this man had suffered liver damage through an illness. After many weeks in hospital he was told that his liver was so badly damaged that he would have to spend the rest of his life with tubes going in and out of his body.

After reading about creative visualization he decided to visualize having a healthy liver. Over the next few months he spent many hours visualizing a process of cleaning his liver, one cell at a time, with an imaginary toothbrush. At first he pictured it as a black blob, but using his imaginary toothbrush he slowly began to clean it and picture it turning a healthy pink colour.

After a few months he had an accident in his home and one of the tubes was torn out of his body. He was rushed to hospital, where the doctors prepared him for an operation. But when he was X-rayed, the surgeon was astonished to discover that his liver had completely regenerated and was in perfect condition.

There are many similar stories of the power of visualization.

To Create and to Cure

As we know, thoughts can also create disease. But most people who fall ill are not even aware of the active role they might have played in the process. If everybody were to know how their thoughts and emotions could create and cure disease then a lot of people would be changing what they were focusing on.

The mind can have an active role in the creation of even the most serious of diseases. One of the major accelerators of cancer, for example, is suppressed negative emotion. While some people have an emotional release valve where they speak to someone about their issues and their pain when necessary, beat a pillow or even shout and curse, others store it all up inside. Over a number of years they might hold in a lot of emotional pain, anxiety, anger, frustration or resentment. Research has shown that there is a relationship between the growth of emotional pain and a tumour growing inside the body when a person has cancer. Please note, however, that this does not mean that suppressed negative emotion *causes* cancer, only that it may speed it up if a person *has* cancer.

In 1989 James Gross, while at the University of California at Berkeley, actually published a summary of 18 individual scientific studies that had been reported in the scientific journals over the previous 30 or so years. This showed a clear link between the suppression of negative emotions and the progression of the cancer in cancer patients.

One of the earliest of the studies dated back to 1954, when researchers studied the personality types of 50 patients and showed how they could be related to the development of various forms of cancer. It was clear that cancer progressed fastest in people who had high levels of anxiety but held it in, pretending that everything was fine, instead of showing their worries or discharging them. The correlation was so clear in this particular study that the scientists were able to accurately predict the rate at which cancer would progress in 78 per cent of people, simply according to their personality type.

A similar study in 1985 described an obvious relationship between the thickness of tumours and what is known as 'nonverbal Type C personality'. Tumours were thickest in this type of people, who were described as being 'co-operative, unassertive and suppressing negative emotion'.

A similar relationship was found between HIV and suppressed emotion. In 1996, scientists at UCLA reported their findings in the journal *Psychosomatic Medicine*. They showed that HIV progressed at a rate that depended upon the degree to which gay men came 'out of the closet'. The scientists studied 80 HIV-positive gay men and discovered that the disease progressed most slowly in those who were open about their sexuality and most quickly in those who weren't. They found that men who were most 'in the closet' reached a critically low immune count 40 per cent faster than the others, developed AIDS 38 per cent faster and reached average mortality 21 per cent faster.

As well as showing the relationship between suppressing negative emotion and ill health, however, these studies also imply that releasing the pain can slow down and even cure serious diseases.

In fact, in 1988 Pennebaker, Kiecolt-Glaser and Glaser published a scientific paper that described a link between the immune system and the release of built-up emotion. When their patients wrote about past thoughts and traumas and thoroughly resolved their feelings about them, their immune systems got stronger.

In 1999 a similar experiment was conducted with asthma and rheumatoid arthritis patients. After writing about stressful experiences over a three-session period, the asthma patients were found to have improved lung function and the rheumatoid arthritis patients to have reduced severity of the disease.

A report in the medical journal *The Lancet* showed that expressing emotion even prolonged the life of cancer patients. This research involved 86 women with metastatic breast cancer who were invited to participate in a therapy where they were able to express stored emotions while being emotionally supported throughout the process. The women who underwent this therapy lived almost twice as much longer as the women who didn't.

Similarly, a 2002 report in the *Journal of Clinical Oncology* invited women who had breast cancer to write about either their deepest thoughts and feelings about a stressful experience or positive thoughts and feelings about their breast cancer experience. After four sessions of 20-minute writing over a three-month period, the women reported significant reductions in negative physical symptoms as well as much-reduced necessity for medical visits.

And in her life-changing book *The Journey*, Brandon Bays described curing herself of a 'basketball-sized' tumour in her abdomen in six weeks, principally through releasing suppressed negative emotion. She described the process as being like peeling off the layers of emotion as if peeling an onion. In a demonstration of the link between mind and body, layers of her tumour peeled off too.

Of course, not everyone who suppresses negative emotion will get cancer, or even become ill. These studies reflect a set of scientific experiments that homed in on a particular area, which is often the case in science. There are a large number of competing factors that can cause cancer and accelerate the course of any disease.

Also, even though there is an obvious link between emotion and the immune system, this does not mean that every time you are emotionally low your immune system will be weakened. Nor does it mean that every time you are happy your immune system will be strengthened. There are many factors that can affect the immune system, and emotion is only one of them.

Occasional anger, for example, is unlikely to cause any heart problems. Despite the evidence of the effects of anger on the heart, even regular anger may not be unhealthy, as it may provide a well-needed emotional release. Conversely, care, compassion or appreciation may not make everyone healthy.

But in general, due to the body-mind relationship, a healthy mind will have a positive influence upon the health of the body. So whatever you can do in your life to improve your mental and emotional health, whether that is adopting a more positive attitude to life, meditating, laughing, choosing to appreciate life, choosing to be more caring and compassionate or talking through any issues and pain with a friend, colleague or therapist, there will most likely be benefits to your health.

The choice is yours!

2

The Power of Faith

If you had a headache and a doctor gave you a pill, telling you that it was a good painkiller, your headache would probably go away shortly after you had taken the tablet. But it wouldn't really matter whether the doctor gave you a painkiller or a potato – if you believed that it was a painkiller, you would get pain relief. This is the 'placebo effect'.

A placebo is a dummy medicine or treatment that has nothing chemical in it that has healing powers. It is usually made to look and feel exactly like the drug being tested, so if, say, the drug is a white tablet with a blue triangle on it then the placebo tablet will also be white with a blue triangle on it.

Placebos are used in lots of medical trials around the world because they are not supposed to heal, therefore any cures that take place can be credited to the medicine being tested. In this way, researchers can prove that the new medicine works. But in practice, people are healed when they take placebos. The effect has been shown to cure anywhere between 10 per cent and 100 per cent of people, depending upon the nature of the trial and the type of illness being studied. For some diseases the placebo effect is low and for others it is high.

Say a medical trial was set up to determine how good a new drug was for colds and 'flu. It might involve 1,000 people. Five hundred of them would get the drug and the other 500 would get the placebo. And so that there would be no special treatment from the medical staff administering the tablets, neither the patients nor the staff would know who was getting what.

During the study, which might run for several months, information about the number and severity of episodes of colds and 'flu would be collected from each person taking part, and then scientists would compare the symptoms of the people who received the drug and the people who received the placebo.

They might find, for instance, that there were fewer symptoms in 400 out of the 500 people who received the drug, but also that there were fewer symptoms in 300 of those who got the placebo. In this case, there would clearly be something in the way that the people on the placebo were thinking or feeling that caused their bodies to heal.

The placebo effect makes you wonder how many of the people who receive a drug in medical trials are actually cured by the placebo effect. Does the drug itself cure them or is it their faith in the drug?

It also makes you wonder how many times in the past your recovery from an illness had more to do with your belief in the medicine, or in the doctor, than in the medicine you were given. This is one of the reasons why a certain drug might work well for one person but not for another – one person might have more faith in it than the other.

In fact snake oil might be a legitimate cure after all. It was great in its day because people believed in it. Some modern drugs are no better or worse.

Some doctors believe that it is important to give a patient a new drug while it is still considered the 'in thing' because once another new drug appears on the scene, the previous one seems to lose much of its miraculous healing power. It's not because the medicine stops working but because people stop believing in it, especially because the new one is likely to be advertised to be an 'all-singing, all-dancing wonder pill'.

Time has revealed that many miraculous medicines of the past had almost no real curative powers of their own. But the patients who believed in them and were cured by them didn't know that at the time. Someone once said to me, 'Aerodynamically, a bumble bee shouldn't be able to fly, but it doesn't know that.' It's just as well!

Taking faith out of the healing equation would nevertheless reveal many medicines to be very powerful, but it is just not possible to remove faith. The bottom line is that if you believe in a particular medicine, or in the doctor who prescribed it, then it is more likely to work for you. Conversely, if you don't believe in the medicine or in the doctor, there is a good chance that you will negate the medicine's power.

Some shamans in remote areas of the world are well aware of the power of an individual to cure themselves and use that as a legitimate part of their 'whole person' treatment. Their ceremonies sometimes give the patient the feeling that they are being given 'the works'. The sick person totally buys into the treatment and their internal curative powers step in to do the work.

However, this is not the only reason why such treatments work. Shamans are also aware of the many herbs and combinations of plant essences that have powerful curative properties. They also use techniques to help them enter a higher state of consciousness where they are able to perceive the deeper mental, emotional and spiritual nature of disease, allowing them to be more specific in their treatment.

Whatever methods are used, traditional or modern, there is more than one pathway to healing in the body. Molecules can move one way or the other during the process of recovery. Faith could cause them to go left and medicine could cause them to go right, but at the end of the day there's a healthy person. The placebo effect is powerful, but so are plant essences, herbs, vitamins, minerals and modern drugs. Caring and compassionate scientists, whose goal is to make a difference in the world, put a lot of dedication and genius into the research and development of new treatments for disease. I should know, because I used to be one of them. Medical researchers nowadays are able to chemically interrupt disease processes in ways that would even astound a rocket scientist.

The point is that there are many different types of medical treatment, but since thoughts, feelings and beliefs are so intimately entangled with the healing process it is probably wisest to go with the one you have most faith in.

Over the past 50 years a large number of scientific investigations have uncovered just how powerful healing can be when you believe in the treatment you are receiving.

Scientific Studies

Lots of research has been done on the placebo effect in recent years. Most scientists agree that it works because of three main factors:

1.   A person's desire to be healed.

2. Their expectancy that they are going to be healed, or that something positive is going to happen.
3. Their belief that they will be healed, either because they believe in the medicine or because they believe in the competency of the medical staff looking after them.

Based upon the evidence discussed throughout this book, I would add another factor: feelings. Expectancy or belief produces feelings. You 'feel' more positive or you 'feel' that you will get better.

The power of faith has been known for a long time. In the Bible it is written:

'... the blind men came to him. And Jesus said to them, "Do you believe that I am able to do this?" They said to him, "Yea, Lord." Then he touched their eyes, saying, "According to your faith, be it unto you." *And their eyes were opened.'* (My emphasis).

Mathew 9:28

Science has since caught up a little with this teaching, revealing in numerous experiments that the degree to which you believe governs the rate at which you are healed. There are now numerous scientific studies on the power of the placebo effect to heal and a growing number of scientists working in the area.

In 2004, for example, Fabrizio Benedetti of the University of Turin School of Medicine in Italy published a scientific report in the journal *Nature Neuroscience* that showed the changes that took place in the brains of people with Parkinson's disease when they believed they were receiving real medicine.

The patients had been receiving drug injections that would reduce symptoms of the disease such as muscle stiffness and tremors. But when they were given a harmless saltwater injection instead but told it was the real drug, their muscles relaxed and they could move more easily.

By measuring electrical signals from individual brain cells, Benedetti showed real changes in areas of the brain that are usually hyperactive in Parkinson's patients.

One of the earliest placebo experiments was performed in 1950. In a scientific report published in the *Journal of Clinical Investigation*, scientists described a powerful placebo effect in a group of 33 pregnant women who were experiencing morning sickness.

The women took part in a trial in which they were told that they would be given a drug that would stop their nausea and vomiting. This is what is called 'suggestion'. It was 'suggested' that the drug would work. To make the results even more precise, the scientists asked the women to swallow a small instrument that would allow them to measure the stomach contractions that came with the waves of nausea.

After they took the drug the women reported that their nausea and vomiting had stopped and the researchers noted that the contractions measured by the swallowed instruments had also stopped. So the drug had been very successful. But actually the women were not given a drug to reduce nausea and vomiting, but one that should have made them even sicker, syrup of ipecac.

So a strong desire to feel better (who wouldn't want to get rid of nausea?) coupled with a belief that a drug would work was able to override the powerful effects of a substance that should have made matters worse. In this instance, the drug should have made the molecules go left, but faith was stronger and made them go right, figuratively speaking.

A similar type of study was conducted on asthma volunteers at the University of London in 1986. They were involved in a trial apparently to test a new drug. First they were told they would be given a substance that would cause their chests to constrict. So when they inhaled it through an inhaler their breathing became more difficult, as you would expect. Then the experiment was repeated, except that the new drug was given before the constricting substance and the volunteers were told that it would protect them from it. In this instance the constricting substance had no effect.

However, in neither case did the inhalers contain any such drugs. They contained water. Yet the volunteers experienced chest constriction and expansion each time they used the inhalers. Their belief that they were inhaling a chest constrictor or a new drug caused their bodies to act appropriately.

A very simple study, but one which clearly revealed the power of belief, was reported in 1996. It compared the effectiveness of capsules of different colours but which, unknown to the volunteers, contained the same substances.

A group of medical students was asked to take either a blue capsule or a pink one and told that the capsules either contained a sedative or a stimulant, although in both cases they were chemically inert; they were placebos. But throughout the study it became apparent that the blue capsules were more powerful sedatives than the pink ones. This was probably because the volunteers associated the colour blue with feeling calm and this brought about a feeling of relaxation in their minds and then their bodies.

Similarly, a study of many different brands of aspirin tablets found that the ones with a red cross on them were the most powerful. Presumably this was because a red cross is usually associated with rescue and the feeling of being safe. This feeling would have caused healing in the body.

In 2002 scientists showed that the power of belief even influences the immune system. Volunteers were repeatedly given a flavoured drink which contained a chemical called cyclosporin A, which is known to suppress the immune system. With each drink, therefore, their immune systems were weakened.

When the volunteers were later given the drink with no cyclosporin added, their immune systems still weakened. Through the repeated association (at an unconscious level) between the drink and a weakened immune system, the drink alone was enough to cause the effect, just as Dr Pavlov caused his dogs to salivate each time he rang a bell.

The power of the placebo effect is easily noticeable in eating and drinking. On a number of occasions I have noticed that people in average health fall ill more often once they start a healthy diet and lifestyle. At first they feel great and their health improves, which is what should happen when a person improves their diet. But problems begin to arise as they learn more about which foods are considered good and which ones are not. Now they look back at what they used to eat with horror, labelling most of it as unhealthy, and whenever they have a slip-up from the healthy diet (which most of us do), eating something they now believe to be unhealthy, they are unconsciously telling themselves, 'I am unhealthy.' Then the body simply reflects the belief as an illness. Previously, before they learned about nutrition, eating that food would not have caused the harm because they didn't know that it was bad for them.

It is sometimes not so much food but our thoughts *about* food that cause us problems. Of course, there are foods that are generally accepted as nutritious and it is wise to eat them. There are also some that are not, and eating lots of those every day might not be very clever. But the body is very resilient. Having chips or chocolate cake occasionally probably isn't going to make much difference to your health.

The problem is that a lot of people dwell on when they ate something fattening or sugary and so send their body lots of 'I am unhealthy' signals, which the body dutifully reproduces, forgetting the fact that almost everything else they ate was highly nutritious. If this happens to you, just keep reminding yourself that if you generally eat nutritious food, the occasional slip-up probably won't do any harm.

Instant Healing

A few years ago, one of my friends had a heavy cold that gave her a headache and a blocked nose and made her feel run down. She had newly joined a charity that a group of friends and I were operating and was aware that we shared a belief in 'hands-on' healing. Quite a few people in the group were practising therapists and at the time I was also doing some therapy work for people, usually family and friends, and as a scientist I was intrigued by how hands-on healing worked.

My friend had never received a treatment, but she really, really, believed in it because she had heard some remarkable stories. She spoke to me about her cold symptoms and I felt genuine compassion for her and offered to help.

I recognized her openness and faith and the fact that she didn't know what a healing treatment consisted of, so I simply placed my hand on her forehead, gave her a little push and said out loud, with directness and conviction, 'Cold, cancel!'

Her nose cleared and her headache vanished immediately!

I hadn't performed any special treatment. I had simply recognized her faith that instant healing was possible and she had done the rest. Her own belief had caused a cascade of biological movements that had made her instantly feel better. Taking a placebo tablet on the understanding that it was a powerful new drug known to have an immediate effect might have had the same result.

Molecules of Emotion

The power of the mind to cure is awesome and scientists have spent considerable time investigating it. In particular, they have studied tiny molecules called neuropeptides, which Professor Candace Pert labelled 'molecules of emotion' in her excellent book of the same name.

The name 'neuropeptide' comes from the fact that these molecules are usually present in the brain (neuro) and that they are made up of peptide units, which are parts of proteins.

The importance of neuropeptides was uncovered as a result of research which took place in the 1970s, when scientists discovered how mind-altering opiates like heroin and morphine worked. A number of scientists made the assumption that for opiates to affect the mind they must interact with areas of the brain that control emotions. Such areas were well known at the time.

As for how it worked, have you ever seen those children's learning toys where there are coloured shapes – usually a square, a triangle, a circle, a star, perhaps a rectangle and some other shapes – and the children are supposed to fit them into holes of the same shape on a small table? Now imagine that when a child puts the correct shape in the hole a green flashing light goes off.

Drugs and other chemicals interface with the brain in the same way. Each has its own hole on the table, or 'receptor' as it's called in biology, and when a drug fits that receptor, instead of a flashing light the body switches on a particular function. In this way, when a drug fits its receptor the body can bring about healing.

A few scientists made the assumption that opiates had a specific 'hole', or receptor, in the brain's emotional areas. When opiates came along and fitted into the hole, emotions were switched on and this was how opiates caused an emotional 'high'.

For a while, the existence of the opiate receptor was merely a theory, but following its discovery in 1972 by Candace Pert and Sol Snyder, while at Johns Hopkins University, the entire field opened up. Scientists reasoned that if these chemical opiates fitted a specific receptor then the body must have its own natural opiate, otherwise why would such a receptor exist?

Research soon uncovered it. It was identified at the University of Aberdeen, in Scotland, by John Hughes and Hans Kosterlitz. It is a neuropeptide called endorphin, a natural opiate that also gives you a high. This is why sportspeople can become addicted to exercise, because endorphins are produced during intense exercise. The high produced can be comparable to that of other addictive opiates.

As well as neuropeptides affecting emotion, emotion also affects the number and type of neuropeptides. So, in typical body-mind fashion, it goes both ways. Neuropeptides switch on emotion and emotion switches on neuropeptides. In mind-body science this is called a 'bi-directional' effect.

It is now understood that neuropeptides are involved in a whole array of different bodily functions, from hormone regulation to protein manufacture, cellular repair upon injury, memory storage and pain management. So, since neuropeptides are produced by emotion, all of these things are affected by how a person feels.

It is now known that there is an entire psychosomatic network connecting the body and mind involving hundreds of neuropeptides and thousands of receptor locations throughout the body. Any of a vast range of thoughts or feelings can cause a whole cascade of changes in a person's body.

Thoughts and feelings basically 'light up' specific areas of the body. Neuropeptides associated with a certain emotion will light up areas where receptors for those neuropeptides are present, changing them in some way. So if receptors for compassion are present in the big toe, then compassion will light up the big toe.

So a 'gut feeling', for instance, is more than just a subjective feeling. It is also a real chemical movement in the gut where neuropeptide receptors are found. The feeling leads to the production of specific neuropeptides in the brain and these light up specific receptors present in the gut, thereby allowing a person to physically feel an instinct.

Many neuropeptides have receptors all over the body, so emotions are physically felt all over the body. Have you ever felt your whole body tingle when you are thinking a certain thought or feeling a certain way, or when an idea just 'clicks'? Neuropeptides are simply fitting into receptors in those parts of your body.

The whole body is psychosomatically wired to dance to the tune of any thought and emotion. Thoughts of care and compassion can induce changes in the immune system because they cause the production of the neuropeptides that light up the receptors found on some immune cells, thereby switching them on. Thoughts of appreciation can induce rhythm changes in the heart because neuropeptides associated with appreciation have receptors in the autonomic nervous system.

Accordingly, when a person experiences pain relief when they take a placebo, the neuropeptides associated with faith (belief, expectancy or feelings brought about by faith) must have receptors in the brain or where the pain is felt.

In the 1970s, scientists began to study this and the proof came in 1978 when scientists from the departments of Neurology, Physiology and Oral Surgery at UC San Francisco published their research in the medical journal *The Lancet*. Since then, many scientific studies have conclusively proven that neuropeptides are responsible for pain relief when a person believes they are receiving medicine.

In 2005 Jon-Kar Zubieta of the University of Michigan took it even further. He obtained PET scans showing exactly what was happening in the brain when a person was receiving a placebo for pain relief.

The study, published in the *Journal of Neuroscience*, involved 14 men who participated in a 'pain challenge' by having saltwater injected into their jaw muscles. After a short time, half of the men were injected with what they believed was an analgesic, although it was secretly a placebo, and their pain was substantially reduced. PET scans of their brains then revealed lots of changes in specific areas of the brain, proving once and for all that the placebo effect was a real physical change and not just a figment of the imagination.

Numerous scientific studies have now proven beyond all doubt that the 'mind over matter' effect is real. What you think about, what you believe and how you feel affect the matter in your body.

Remember that if you had a headache and the doctor gave you a potato, telling you it was a good painkiller, your headache would have probably gone away? If they had really given you a painkiller, that would have worked by fitting into your pain receptors, but the potato would have worked too because your faith in it would have produced natural neuropeptides which would also have fitted into your pain receptors.

Again, this is not to imply that medicines don't work. I have studied the science of how some of them work, so I can assure you that they can be very powerful. But we all have the ability to produce the same results through our faith.

Faith, hope and determination can make a profound difference in the healing process. They might cure you completely, depending upon how much you can muster, or they might only make a small difference. But even a small difference is better than no difference. It might be all you need.

One of the obstacles to healing is not realizing the part you can play. Society leads us to believe that we must always seek cures outside ourselves, dismissing 'mind over matter' as nonsense, but such a belief negates the body's natural healing process. Believing that we need to be cured often stops the body from making its own effortless recovery.

So beliefs can make a medicine work or neutralize it. Perhaps one day, when our faith is super strong, we will transcend the need for medicines altogether. But for now it is wise to take whichever medicine your doctor recommends.

However, our understanding of the bodymind is growing every day. We are now recognizing that even DNA, the building block of life and holder of the genetic code, dances to the tune of the mind.

3
DNA

DNA is frequently in the news at the moment amid reports of cloning and the genetic modification of foods. Cloning is where scientists copy the genetic code found in DNA and produce a genetically identical animal or plant. Dolly the sheep was born from a cloned genetic code. Modifying the code would produce something that was similar yet different – a normal-looking grain that was resistant to infection, for instance. This is typical of some of the research that has been done on GM foods.

But while all of this research has been going on, a new area of DNA research called psychosocial genomics has emerged. A blend of psychology and genomics, its essence is that your DNA is influenced by how you think and feel. But before we go into that, here is a little lesson on DNA.

DNA is short for 'deoxyribonucleic acid', so you may understand why people prefer to call it DNA. Scientists have known for years that it has a double-helix structure, from the work of Crick, Watson and Wilkins, who received a Nobel Prize, and Rosalind Franklin, which was published back in 1953.

Can you picture a spring in your mind? Say, a bedspring or a child's slinky spring? But instead of it being made of a single line of wire, imagine that a railway line has been coiled into a spring so there are two lines. Imagine that just like a railway, there are slats connecting the two strands. The two strands connected by the slats form a double helix. That's what DNA looks like.

The human genome project that you may have heard about was an international research programme set up to crack the genetic code. Scientists wanted to know the exact chemical make-up of DNA.

You have probably heard of genes. Each gene is a small section of DNA whose presence causes you to have a particular physical characteristic, like eye colour or hair colour, for instance. Imagine them as light bulbs. A coil of several thousand of them make up your DNA. In the human genome project, scientists wanted to know the exact sequence of light bulbs, as in which bulb came first, second, third, and so on.

Bet you didn't know that approximately 99.9 per cent of genes are the same for every person on Earth. In other words, you and I have almost identical genes. Most people are under the impression that our genes are very different and having, say, brown hair means that a person must have the brown hair gene and having green eyes means having the green eyes gene. This makes logical sense but it is not entirely correct. Many of the differences between people at birth actually have little to do with whether they have specific genes or not, given that we all have almost the same genes. The differences are mostly due to tiny variations in single genes.

Using the light bulb analogy, a single bulb could represent each gene, but if you were to look inside each bulb you would see that its element was made of a further thousand smaller bulbs. Scientists believe that the main differences between individuals are in the colour of just one of these thousand smaller bulbs inside a single gene. These variations are called single nucleotide polymorphisms (SNPs) and about three million are believed to exist.

However this is only part of the story, because after birth, differences begin to emerge due to specific genes switching on in some people and off in others. Imagine a row of 10 light bulbs. I might have bulbs 2, 4, 6, and 7 switched on and the rest off, while you might have bulbs 4 and 6 switched off but bulb 8 switched on. In the human genome it is a little more complicated, with around 25,000 genes, but the light-bulb analogy is a good one.

There are a number of factors that cause genes to switch on and off, including the normal workings of the body, diet and even exercise, but throughout life our numerous experiences and, more importantly, how we think and feel *about* these experiences, also cause genes to switch on and off. Say you have a meeting with someone. How you feel about them and what you think about them afterwards will determine whether certain genes switch on or off.

So our thoughts and feelings produce significant biological differences between us. Learning has been proven to do this too. Differences in what each person learns lead to differences in which genes are on and which are off, which in turn lead to differences in the growth of the brain and differences in the body due to the bodymind connection.

The activation of genes is also a significant reason for the differences between us and other species of life (although we are hardly likely to mutate into another species). For example, there is a 98.5 per cent similarity between our genes and those of chimpanzees. Similarly, 57 per cent of our genes are shared with a cabbage, 51 per cent with yeast, 50 per cent with the worm and 30 per cent with the banana. Unbelievable but true! The differences are mostly down to which genes are naturally on and which ones are off, and how long they are on or off for.

Our bodies are mostly composed of proteins, which are constructed when genes switch on. They are the building blocks of our bodies, just as bricks are the building blocks of a house. So, between species, most of the same proteins are present but they are produced at different times and in different amounts. Therefore, just as the same set of bricks could be used to build a variety of different shapes and sizes of buildings, the same set of genes can produce an infinite variety of species.

Influencing our Genes

The effect of our thoughts and feelings on our genes raises the question of how far we can influence our genes.

It seems that the effect varies between genes. In some cases, genetics (nature) might contribute around 50 per cent of a person's make-up, both physical and psychological, although this number varies depending upon a person's age and the physical, physiological or behavioural trait in question. The remaining 50 per cent would be open to the influence of the environment (nurture), which includes diet and lifestyle as well as thoughts and feelings. However, it is very difficult to attach percentages to this because there is a constant interplay between 'nature' and 'nurture'. So genetics plays a significant role, but so does life experience. Both nature and nurture are important.

For instance, if two people inherited almost identical genes – identical twins, for instance – but lived in different environments and were exposed to different diets and life experiences, they would probably grow up to be different heights. Scientific studies involving identical twins have in fact shown that height is around 80 per cent heritable (a measure of the relative genetic influence) and the remaining 20 per cent is open to the environment. So while two people may have inherited the same predisposition to be tall, their diets and daily experiences will be the deciding factor as to what height they actually end up.

Almost any particular attribute or state of health could be changed, perhaps, with the aid of willpower and faith. I believe that the question is not whether such a thing is possible or not, but how much willpower and faith are required.

Genes and Visualization

In a 1998 scientific paper Professor Eric Kandel, year 2000 Nobel Prizewinner in Medicine, pointed out that all bodily functions are susceptible to how we interact with life. His research focused upon how memories are stored in the brain.

When you experience something – say, meeting a new person or even something as simple as enjoying a meal – it is stored in the brain as a memory, forming neural connections or, depending upon the intensity of the experience, forming brain cells (neurons) in a process known as neurogenesis.

Intense experiences like those of artistic or spiritual nature, or ones accompanied by a high emotional charge like excitement, fascination, wonder, awe or enthusiasm, produce neurons, whereas normal everyday experiences produce simple neural connections. You could picture it as intense experiences producing balls and normal experiences producing thin fibres.

But in each case it is not so much the experience itself but our thoughts and feelings *about* the experience that cause this.

So when something significant happens, our thoughts and feelings about it switch on genes that construct whatever proteins or cellular components are required for its storage as a memory in the brain, biologically encoding it so to speak. (I personally believe that memories are not just stored in the brain but that they have an equivalent all throughout the body, since the entire body is hardwired to feel every emotion. It's just that science hasn't looked anywhere else yet.) Any experience that is mentally and emotionally significant forms a strong long-lasting memory because it is played over and over in the mind. As it is replayed, the genes repeatedly express their information, building up an indelibly etched memory, or biological equivalent, which can be a neuron if the experience is significant enough.

Think of a time when you had a powerful experience – a first date, for instance. Did you think about it for hours afterwards, even days? Did you daydream about it, even make up extra stuff in your mind? Of course you did. It is this creative replaying, or daydreaming, that causes the repetitive gene expression (the switching on of the light bulb over and over and over again) that eventually produces neurons and neural connections. And if you think about it, replaying, or daydreaming, is visualization.

So in other words visualization (including the feelings associated with the images) inspires genes to switch on, causing the growth of proteins and cells. The more you visualize, and the stronger the emotional charge accompanying the images, the brighter the light bulb becomes and the more proteins and cells you construct.

You might now understand why it was possible for the man mentioned earlier to completely regenerate his liver. His repetitive visualization undoubtedly switched on specific genes that caused the construction of healthy liver cells.

In fact our intentional and unintentional visualization inspires DNA 24 hours a day, 365 days a year. We are simply unaware of the process. So we continually affect our genetic code and the nature of the effect is largely down to the nature of our thoughts, feelings, attitudes, beliefs and intentions.

Put this into perspective in relation to health. When we are ill we tend to dwell on the illness, which is normal because illness is usually unpleasant and difficult to forget about. But in thinking about it, it is likely that we are actually helping to build new cells with a memory of disease. Our mental images and their associated feelings of gloom will switch on specific genes that build up diseased cells in our bodies.

On the other hand, if we release our emotional pain through talking with someone or having some sort of therapy, then begin to dwell on positive, appreciative thoughts and feelings, we will encourage the growth of healthy cells. This is why hypnosis has been shown to be a powerful tool in the healing arts and it is possibly also why releasing suppressed negative emotion can send cancer into regression.

In fact, it has been theorized that spontaneous remission from cancer, where it vanishes virtually overnight, is a switching on of the interleukin-2 gene as a result of tremendous faith, hope, determination, visualization, a complete change of belief system or some other powerful experience. When turned on, this gene turbo-charges the immune system, causing a neutralization of cancer cells and other harmful pathogens. So even if a person has inherited a tendency for an oncogene (cancer gene) to be switched on, a significant change of mind could switch it off, rendering the person healed.

If a person inherits an SNP (a tiny variation in a gene) that produces a disease, I believe that it is possible that, with willpower and faith, they can create a new 'program' to switch genes on and off and cancel it out.

This is not to say that it would be easy to do so. It simply means that it is possible. Our current understanding of this process is primitive, but it *does* suggest that such things *are* possible and that there is probably a way to perform such miracles at will. Some individuals may unconsciously do it all the time. Perhaps it will be more commonplace at some point in the future.

Genes and Love

One of the most powerful effects of heart and mind on DNA that has been reported to date in the scientific journals is the effect of love, or lack of it.

In 2003 and 2005, scientists showed that gently brushing rat pups for 15 minutes a day during their first week of life altered the activation of specific genes so that the pups grew up to have a better memory, improved mental abilities and a better ability to deal with stress.

In 1995, while also studying rat pups, researchers had showed that when a mother's touch was deprived there was a dramatic reduction in the levels of important growth hormones in the infants' bodies. Growth hormones are the substances that cause cells, organs and individual body parts to grow, so they are of prime importance in the bodies of children.

The researchers studied two genes called c-myc and c-max, which switch on a gene called ornithine decarboxylase (ODC) that is involved in the construction of growth hormones in the body. Maternal touch promotes the activation of c-myc and c-max, leading to normal growth of an infant.

However, the researchers discovered that if maternal touch was deprived for 10 or 15 minutes there was a significant drop in ODC gene expression, which went down to 40 per cent within two hours. Forty per cent! That's a massive drop in growth-hormone levels. In other words, deprivation of touch has a stunting effect on growth.

This might give you an idea of the importance of love. A mother's touch makes an infant feel loved and the love promotes its growth. When there is no loving touch, the infant experiences feelings of fear (the absence of love) and this suppresses its growth.

Love promotes growth and fear suppresses it!

A number of social workers investigating neglected children have actually reported coming across abnormally small children who were later found to have extremely low levels of growth hormones and to have difficulty 'fitting in'. The feelings experienced by the children presumably switched off c-myc and c-max, thereby slowing the growth process. The condition is known as 'psychosocial dwarfism' or 'non-organic failure-to-thrive'.

Please note, however, that a person's size, in general, is not an indicator of how much love they received as a child. As we learned previously, around 80 per cent of height is in the genes. Only 20 per cent is influenced by environment and life experiences. The point is merely that the genes are *influenced* by love and fear.

And before you start worrying about laying your infant down for a short time, the scientists also discovered that if maternal touch was resumed then ODC over-expressed by a factor of 300 per cent, producing elevated amounts of growth hormones as if to make up for lost time. Nature, it seems, is not without a sense of balance.

Infants also benefit from a range of experiences that don't always involve direct touch from a parent, for example when they are playing with toys. So it seems as though nature has built this overcompensation into the process of evolution.

Some researchers have actually discovered that a positive, loving environment in the home is ideal. While studying the brain, they learned that the area known as the prefrontal lobes, at the front of the head just above the eyes, grows more pronounced if a child is brought up in a positive, loving environment. When a child is consistently deprived of love there can be a stunting effect on its growth and the prefrontal lobes don't develop fully. A well-developed set of prefrontal lobes is associated with a person being able to express themselves comfortably, being emotionally well adjusted and being spiritually aware. A child with underdeveloped prefrontal lobes often has difficulty with emotional expression later in life.

However, some of these effects can be reversed through love and care. A 2003 report in the journal *Neuroscience* showed that some of the negative effects on the brain of lack of love in early childhood could be reversed through good nurturing.

Genes and Determination

So, we are rarely stuck with a 'bad set of genes', so to speak.

Learning and practice can offset any setbacks we might have experienced and can also enhance our natural abilities. And as we learn and practise, our thoughts and feelings switch on genes that help us to master whatever we are focusing upon. Similarly, our general state of health can be improved when we are determined to recover from an illness or when we are visualizing ourselves well.

My mum enjoyed jumping when she was a child. She loved jumping so much that she became really good at the high jump as a teenager and performed excellently at the county sports championships. For years afterwards she talked about jumping over the clothes line in her back garden every evening and the joy she felt from it. I was often moved by the excitement in her voice as she vividly recounted these experiences, acting out the jumping motions on the sitting-room floor.

As I grew up I loved to watch athletics on TV with my family, particularly the Olympic Games. Inspired by my mum, I would often daydream about being an athlete and competing in a major championship. In my mid-twenties I tried out for the sprint team in a large UK athletics club called Sale Harriers Manchester, but although I was quite fast I wasn't good enough to make the team.

A few days later I was at the track by myself, playing around at jumping into the sandpit. After several jumps the head of the club approached me. He had been watching me and wondered who I was, because I was a new face at the track. He asked how far I could jump, so I paced out my last jump and said it looked to be about 6.5 metres, which is about 21.5 feet. He was visibly impressed and asked me to come to the track the following evening because that's when the long-jump squad trained under the coaching of Terry Davidson. He wanted me to join the club as a long jumper, so I did. And I became very good at it.

Within a month or two, under Terry's coaching, I was one of the top long jumpers in Scotland, but prior to Sale Harriers Manchester I had never done a day's formal jump training in my life. Most of my training had been mental and emotional daydreaming.

There is most likely a 'jumping gene' or a set of genes that motivate a person to want to jump and thus develop stronger and more elastic muscles. I may have been born with favourable genetics, but then again I may not. The right genes might have simply been turned on because of the thoughts, feelings and motivation I was exposed to through my mum's love of jumping. These mental and emotional experiences would have written a new genetic program, switching on specific genes that caused my muscles to develop and perform in an appropriate way. My ability would therefore have been independent of whether I had inherited 'athletic genes' or not.

When a person is highly motivated, genes switch on, brain cells grow and proteins are manufactured so that the person begins to evolve into the image of themselves that they are striving to become.

If you think about it, it is doubtful that every Olympic medallist will have been born with 'athletic genes'. But I believe that numerous genes will have been encouraged to become switched on through the athletes' sheer determination and willpower.

All of us have the capacity to become pretty much anything we desire because we have all of the genes in the gene pool and they are all susceptible to mental and emotional influences. The question is simply, what are you motivated to become?

There are probably no limits to what any of us can be. All of us have the 'Olympic athlete gene' waiting to be expressed, and the 'great artist', 'sculptor', 'musician', 'actor, 'scientist', 'writer', 'teacher', 'peacemaker', 'lover', 'parent', 'genius' and 'healer gene'. It's all in your DNA, just waiting for you to want it and have the faith that you can be it.

Many people's latent abilities are obstructed by their belief that they can't do something. Who says you can't? You can! Everyone can live their dreams, regardless of past conditions or the performances of family members. Anyone can have the desire and a little faith, and that might be all that is needed.

Look to what's in your heart!

4
The Power of Intention

Scientific journals contain hundreds of research papers that show that we can use mental techniques to affect both our own bodies and those of other people. As we have already learned, thoughts of appreciation, care and compassion can smooth the rhythms of the heart and elevate the immune system, and even our genes dance to the tune of our hopes and dreams.

We can also use mental techniques like visualization to speed up healing in any area of the body. The results of visualization are not always obvious, because many people are looking for the 'instant fix'. Most think that if they visualize themselves in good health an illness should go away right away. It should! But there are very few people whose beliefs are strong enough to make it so.

Instead many of us do the opposite. We believe that it isn't possible for the illness to disappear right away just as strongly as we believe it is possible and, like a negative placebo effect (the nocebo effect), this interferes with the healing process. We end up taking two steps back for every three we take forward and eventually the stronger belief wins. The result is that visualization only *appears* to have small effects. But even so, a small effect is better than no effect.

No matter what ache, pain or illness you might experience, intend to get better. Determination coupled with hope and faith can move mountains. The placebo effect clearly shows that the body has the ability to heal if we believe it can.

Our thoughts and feelings can affect other people's bodies too. Have you ever noticed that if you are in a bad mood you quickly affect the mood of everyone around you? The same is true when you are in a good mood.

Scientific research has actually proven that a good mood is infectious. Publishing in the *Journal of Nonverbal Behaviour* in 1981, Howard Friedman and Ronald Riggio found that when a person in a good mood (as determined by a score on a questionnaire) sat facing a person with a lower score for two minutes, their mood was transmitted. The person with the lower score felt better.

If you affect a person's mood then you also affect their biology, given that the body and mind are intertwined. In this way, then, you can intentionally affect someone's health in a positive way.

For example, if you generate a warm feeling of appreciation for a person when you are in their company, imagining, perhaps, a time when they said or did something nice, they will pick it up from you and their feelings will have healing effects throughout their body. The same happens when you say something nice or do something kind for another person. In a very real sense a loving intention heals.

A loving touch also makes a big difference. We have seen that a mother lovingly stroking her infant will switch on genes that help it to grow and switch off genes that produce stress hormones. It is likely that a similar thing occurs with adults, aiding their growth and repair process and reducing stress.

Over the last few years there has been a rapid rise in the number of practitioners of healing touch techniques. In fact in some countries there are far more practitioners of techniques like Therapeutic Touch and Reiki than there are doctors.

Such practitioners are trained to place their hands on or just above an area to be healed. Many use visualization techniques while others simply trust that healing is taking place. I know a number of people who have testified to feeling incredibly relaxed during and after a healing session and whose physical, mental, emotional or spiritual condition has cleared up shortly afterwards.

Anyone can perform healing on another person. Proper training can teach anatomy, physiology and diagnosis, medical science and ethics, but anyone can help another person by simply gently stroking, massaging or embracing them. Even compassionately willing them to recover can make a big difference.

This happens all the time, only we rarely notice the role our intentions played, instead putting recoveries down to specific medicines, food or even luck. Of course, medical treatment and nutrition will have had a powerful effect, but so, too, will your intentions.

However, please note that at some point in a person's life it will just be 'their time' and all you can hope for is to give them some comfort in the final stages of their life.

To focus your intentions you can actively visualize a person in perfect health. You can even put your hands on them while imagining this. All that is required is compassion, a willingness to help and a little faith that you might indeed be helping in some way. On an ethical note, I prefer to always ask a person's permission before I do this.

Scientists have studied some of the healing touch therapies and have proven how effective they can be.

In the 1960s, for instance, Dr Bernard Grad of McGill University in Montreal measured the effects of healing touch on mice. He asked a healer named Oscar Estebanay to place his hands every day upon individual goitrous mice in a selected group to see if he could speed up healing in those mice relative to others that he wasn't to perform healing upon. Over the course of the study Dr Grad found that Mr Estebanay had indeed slowed down the rate of development of goitre in the mice that he touched.

In a similar way he studied the effects of Mr Estebanay's touch on the rate of healing of skin wounds on mice. After daily healing treatments the wounds closed up much faster.

In 1972 the same healer was involved in a study that looked at the effect of healing touch on some enzymes held in a jar. Enzymes are molecules that the body uses to transform one substance into another. Many enzymes are involved in digesting food, for example, breaking it down into other substances that the body can use. The study found that daily healing treatments on the enzyme trypsin, over a three-week period, improved its performance in converting substances.

A study conducted in 1999 by Toni Bunnell at the University of Hull studied the effect of healing touch on an enzyme called pepsin. Over a series of 20 trials, she found that the healer speeded up the rate that it carried out its converting.

Similarly, a 1984 study looked at the effects of healing on the mutation of live bacteria, something that occurs quite naturally in the human body. The bacteria Escherichia coli, or

E-coli as it is more commonly known, mutates from one strain, known as *lac*-negative, into another strain, *lac*-positive. Fifty-two people were involved in the study and were given nine tubes each, containing a mixture of both the negative and positive strains. Each person was to hold the tubes in their hands then try to mentally speed up mutation in three tubes, slow down mutation in another three and leave the last three alone to serve as controls.

The results were highly significant. The researchers discovered that the tubes where the subjects had tried to speed up mutation had much more *lac*-positive E-coli than the control samples. The subjects had speeded up the mutation. There was also much less *lac*-positive E-coli in the tubes where the subjects had attempted to slow down mutation.

Healing at a distance has also been studied. A 2004 study jointly performed by the California Pacific Medical Center, the Institute of Noetic Sciences and MD Anderson Cancer Center at the University of Texas found that practitioners of the technique known as qigong were able to influence human-cultured brain cells held a minimum distance of 10 cm from their bodies. Each practitioner directed healing intentions towards the cells for 20 minutes and was able to increase the rate of growth of the cells.

Healing also works with plants. In one of Dr Grad's experiments, he damaged a set of barley seeds by watering them with saltwater. Half of them, however, received saltwater that had been held for a few moments by a healer. Dr Grad then dried the seeds in an oven and watered them every day with ordinary water. At the end of the experiment he discovered that the seeds that had been watered with the saltwater held by the healer had grown much faster than the seeds that had been watered with 'unhealed' saltwater. Somehow there had been a transfer of energy from the healer to the water and it was able to cancel out the damaging effects of the saltwater.

You have probably heard of the 'old wives' tale' that talking to your plants makes them grow better. Scientific evidence shows that this tale should be taken quite literally.

In his book *Autobiography of a Yogi*, Paramahansa Yogananda describes some of the work of Luther Burbank. Yogananda noticed that Mr Burbank's garden had cactus plants with no thorns and this intrigued him. When they were first planted, he was told, the cacti did have thorns, but Mr Burbank spoke kindly and tenderly to them on a regular basis, explaining to them that they didn't need their thorns any more because he harboured no intentions of ever harming them. Gradually the cacti gave up their thorns!

I once visited my friends Andrea, Seth, Kenny and Pamela and was quite impressed by the abnormal size of some of the plants on their windowsill. Andrea told me that she had been giving them Reiki treatments every day since they were seeds. It had clearly helped their growth.

I am sure that many of you reading this right now have noticed that your plants grow better when you are kind to them. It's just the same with people. Every day most of us come into contact with lots of people – family members, colleagues, friends and strangers. There is clear scientific evidence that our thoughts about them have an effect upon them. Do you appreciate other people or do you harbour anger or resentment towards them?

I have noticed that I can sometimes effortlessly change the atmosphere in a room simply by thinking how much I appreciate each person there and then feeling the appreciation.

Quite often there's a profound transformation right before my eyes. A cold or even openly hostile environment can be transformed into a warm, loving, happy, peaceful or forgiving one.

A kind thought, a smile or a few genuinely kind words cost nothing, but they can go a very long way.

Go with the Flow

Exactly how healing works is not scientifically understood at present. It is likely that the act of touch stimulates nerves and sends neuropeptides and other hormones around the body. But studies where no touch was involved suggest that something else is going on too. These studies seem to show that there is a flow of energy through the air from the healer to the organism or patient. And this flow of energy is affected by intentions.

This knowledge is quite new in the West but it has been well known for thousands of years in the East. Ancient healing traditions in China and India, for instance, are based upon the flow of vital and health-giving energy around the body. This energy is known by many names in many cultures, but the most common are: *qi* ('chee'), *prana* and life-force.

These traditions teach that the body requires *qi* to function. A healthy body contains lots of *qi* flowing smoothly throughout, just as blood flows through veins. When a person is ill, the flow of *qi* might be blocked, just as a body would become ill if blood flow were blocked. It is well known that a blockage in the blood flow to the heart, for instance, can cause a heart attack. In the same way, a blockage in the flow of *qi* can bring on a whole range of illnesses by depriving an organ of its vital energy.

Think of it this way: if you were to build a dam on a river, blocking it, then people who needed water downstream would not get enough to drink and to nourish their crops. In the same way, if the flow of *qi* along a particular 'river', or 'meridian' as it is called, is blocked then any organ that usually receives *qi* from that meridian will not get the supply it needs so its health will suffer.

Accordingly, to heal an organ that is not getting enough *qi*, you would need to remove the blockage. This is what acupuncture and many other complementary and alternative therapies try to do. Acupuncturists place needles on meridians at specific locations, known as 'acupuncture points', to stimulate the flow of *qi* so that it dissolves the blockages.

Up until recently Western science hadn't accepted the existence of acupuncture points or meridians, but relatively recent scientific studies have changed that outlook. Even though microscopes can't see acupuncture points, scientists have measured 10 to 20-fold differences in electrical resistance on acupuncture points compared to other points only a centimetre or two away. They have also discovered different amounts of key chemicals at these points. They have even injected radioactive substances into acupuncture points and then followed their flow around the body, creating a map which was found to be identical to the ones drawn up by ancient Chinese and Vedic practitioners.

Earlier we learned that emotions can be stored anywhere in the body, because neuropeptides associated with emotions have receptors all over the body. We also now know that storing emotional pain can cause disease. Stores of negative emotion, then, may block the natural flow of *qi* to an organ or other body part just as a storage of, say, fat or cholesterol may block blood flow to the heart. Expressing and resolving suppressed negative emotions must also, therefore, clear the *qi* blockages.

Qi blockages can also be removed by any medical treatment or therapy that restores the natural flow. This often causes a release of previously blocked emotion, just as unblocking a dam would result in a sudden deluge of water downstream. This is why acupuncture and other energy therapies like Reiki or Shen sometimes cause patients to laugh or cry.

Several years ago I had an acupuncture treatment at a time in my life when I was having difficult mental and emotional challenges. As is normal at such times I was taking life very seriously, perhaps a bit too seriously, and forgetting to see the lighter side. After a few minutes of having needles placed in me I began to laugh. I don't think I'd laughed for several weeks before then, so it was quite a relief. As the treatment removed a blockage of *qi* it also cleared a blockage of emotion that I had stored up. The acupuncture treatment was a highly beneficial and well-needed therapy.

A simple exercise that I have found useful in clearing blockages is as follows:

> Joining my hands together in the prayer position, I focus my attention on my left hand and try to become aware of what it feels like.
>
> I then mentally move that feeling up through the wrist, up the forearm to the elbow. Then I move it up the bicep to the shoulder, along to the neck, through the neck to the right shoulder, then down the right side to the right hand and through to the left hand as the circuit begins again.

> When I've done several circuits I then mentally move
> the flow anywhere in my body, through any blockages or
> areas where there are problems.

What I am doing is becoming aware of *qi* in my body and mentally encouraging its movement to where I want it to go. This technique can be used to direct energy and healing to any diseased or painful part of the body.

Some healing techniques, like this one, guide *qi* to flow through blockages in the hope that the passage of energy might unblock them, just as the rapid flow of water along a blocked pipe, for example, might dislodge the debris that is blocking it.

A scientific study into stroke investigating qigong, a practice that uses intention to direct *qi* around the body, was performed over a 30-year period and involved 242 hypertensive patients. Half of the patients performed 30 minutes of qigong twice daily and the other half did not.

The number of patients who experienced a stroke in the group which didn't practise qi-gong was around 40 per cent (there is a well-known link between hypertension and stroke). But in a clear demonstration of the power of qigong, in the group which practised it the figure was only 20 per cent. Regular practice had halved the number of patients having a stroke.

An additional bonus of the experiment was that the group which practised qigong used their medication less and 30 per cent of them stopped their medication altogether.

Another research project showed that qigong was of enormous benefit to people with cancer. It involved 120 cancer patients, 90 of whom practised two hours of qigong a day for three to six months. During the course of the study all patients received medication for the cancer.

In the qigong-practising group physical strength increased by 80 per cent, yet by only 10 per cent in the other group. Appetite increased in 60 per cent of the group who regularly practised qigong, but only in 10 per cent in the non-qigong group. Following this, a significant weight gain was measured in 60 per cent of the qigong group but in only 15 per cent of the non-qigong group. Lastly, the strength of the immune system increased by 15 per cent in the qigong group but decreased by 20 per cent in the group which didn't practise qigong.

It is likely that the practice of qigong helped to unblock some suppressed emotion as well as increase the amount of vital energy being supplied to all of the organs.

It's Nice to Be Nice

Intention is very powerful. We intend things throughout the day, though mostly we are not even aware of it. But every one of our intentions goes somewhere. Quite likely, if we are thinking of a specific person, it will be going right to them, just as healing intentions will go right where we want it to in our bodies.

This is good if our intentions are kind, compassionate, appreciative or even uplifting, because we will be helping ourselves or another person in some way, but how often do we slip into thinking about how someone has offended us or hurt us in some way, or how we disapprove of their behaviour? What effect do you think your intentions will be having then?

It can do more good to find it in yourself to forgive people, or to accept them just as they are, rather than to send harmful intentions to them. How would you feel if you knew that someone was judging you unfairly without knowing the 'real' you, or thinking angry thoughts about you because of something you might or might not have meant to do?

Every person you have ever interacted with might be a good father or mother, husband or wife, son or daughter or friend, and is dearly loved by someone, just as you are. The way you might have experienced them is not who they really are, it is just how you have experienced them. You will probably never know the real reasons why they behaved that way at that time. And you have probably behaved less than perfectly on at least one occasion of your life. So try to be fair to people. Remember, what you give out always comes back to you in one form or another.

Being genuinely good to people is a good way to improve your overall health too. My dear friend Margaret McCathie, after suffering years of depression and even attempting suicide, was told by Dr Patch Adams (known for the Hollywood film *Patch Adams*), 'Go out and serve and see your depression lift.' She did so and within a few months her depression had indeed lifted. She is now a professional laughter therapist, inspiring others to find their inner joy through service, laughter and kindness. The effect she has on people is extraordinary. The gift of joy she gave to people was returned to her, not only lifting her out of depression but also helping her to develop into an abundant embodiment of happiness.

5
Good Vibrations

Dr Grad's experiments with barley seeds clearly showed that energy had been transferred somehow into water. Since then scientists have studied how water changes in accordance with thoughts and emotions. For instance, Professor William Tiller, Emeritus Professor of Materials Science at Stanford University, has analysed water that has had a person focus intention towards it or even feel strong emotions in the vicinity, and has detected changes in its pH.

In a glass of water the atoms (H-O-H) vibrate, constantly coming together and bouncing apart. They also bend, stretch, spin, twist and collide with other molecules. Other scientists have measured changes in some of these movements when a healer has placed their hands upon the water.

All of these results suggest that your own thoughts and feelings affect water, altering its vibrations. You might want to think a few kind thoughts the next time you are about to drink a glass of water. Could it be that your intentions will colour it and you will nourish your body in a way you might never have imagined?

During a Thanksgiving meal with some friends a few years ago, including Dr Glen Rein of the Quantum Biology Research labs in New York, a talented scientist who conducted some of the Institute of Heartmath's research, I learned that Dr Rein had even placed DNA in a jar containing water that had been held or focused upon and had detected subtle changes in its conformation.

Imagine you are sitting cross-legged on a chair and someone switches on a heater in the room. It gets so warm that you feel uncomfortable, so you change your position and place your feet flat on the floor. Dr Rein showed that DNA changes the way it 'sits' when it is placed in water that a healer has held or focused upon. This is called 'changes in conformation' of DNA.

Our bodies are composed of about 70 per cent water and contain thousands of miles of DNA. This research suggests that both might be affected by what we think about and how we feel.

Also, our intentions towards other people will affect the water in their bodies and their DNA. Of course the effects are very small and subtle. Loving a person may not enlighten them and a dislike of a person is not going to switch on genes that make them grow an extra arm out of their forehead. But continued intentions may build up over time just as, say, trace chemical contaminants in food build up over time and can have toxic consequences.

On the positive side, consistently kind and appreciative intentions towards people will have a long-term beneficial effect upon them. It might make a little difference or it might make a lot, but even a little difference in the right direction is better than a little difference in the wrong direction. What are your intentions towards people?

Given the effects of thoughts and feelings on water, you can even use it as a programmable medicine. For instance, you could write the word 'appreciation' on a label and stick it onto a bottle or glass of water before you drink from it. The word will unconsciously trigger a thought or emotion in you, however small, every time you drink from it and this will 'colour' the water and probably inspire internal coherence in your body.

It might also make you feel more appreciative towards yourself or others. You could try it with 'love', 'peace', 'happiness', 'joy', 'forgiveness', 'passion', 'kindness', or even 'healing' if you want to bring more healing into your body. Be creative! Any quality of intention you wish to add to your body can be written on a label and stuck to a bottle or glass. The effects may be subtle or significant!

Chemical Imprints on Water

Some aspects of homoeopathic medicine and vibrational medicine utilize the transfer of energy into water. Plant essences, Bach Flower Remedies for example, fall into this category because they rely, in part, on the vibrations (bending, stretching, spinning, twisting) of the substances extracted from the plants being transferred into water.

Manufacture of these medicines uses homoeopathic 'succussion' techniques where the plant leaf or flower is boiled up then diluted with water or alcohol. It is then shaken vigorously while a series of successive dilutions are made. Each episode of shaking, or succussion, is believed to 'imprint' the vibrational energy of the leaf or flower onto the water.

The image of certain flowers and plants also brings about a degree of symbolism and emotion, and it is believed that this emotional energy is also imprinted on the water.

The same kind of thing has been done with rocks or crystals that have been shown to possess paramagnetic qualities or are believed to absorb *qi* or intention. Shaking the rocks, or ground-up chunks of them, in water and making successive dilutions is believed to imprint the magnetism or *qi* on the water, producing medicines that can have significant health-enhancing effects upon the body and even on plants.

In some 'rough' and unpublished experiments of my own I have found that some rocks and crystals (particularly ground-up rose quartz) accelerate the rate of germination and growth of cress seeds. If they do this to seeds, there's a good chance that there will be effects on the human body too.

Some therapists imprint water with loving intentions through holding it while focusing on a feeling of genuine love and 'concentrating' it through successive dilutions. When a patient drinks the water, they then receive a concentrated burst of love at a deep level in their body, often with miraculous results.

One of the real advantages of this type of medicine is that the effects go beyond the physical body and can heal emotions and spiritual challenges, which are frequently the underlying causes of disease in the body.

Relatively recent accidental research provided scientific proof of the power of vibrational medicine. During research into allergies, the late Professor Jacques Benveniste, then research director at the French National Institute for Health and Medical Research, was studying the effect of chemical solutions of allergens on the white blood cells of the immune system.

A chemical solution is basically a substance dissolved in water, alcohol or some other solvent. For example, a chemical solution of salt would be a spoonful of salt in a glass of water. A chemical solution of allergens is allergens dissolved in water or dissolved in water plus something else like alcohol.

However, one of Benveniste's students accidentally over-diluted a solution so much that, theoretically, it should not have been able to do anything to the immune system because there weren't enough allergen molecules left in it. In fact it was eventually diluted so much that there was no theoretical possibility of there being even a single molecule of allergen present, so it should have had no effect on the white blood cells whatsoever. Yet it did – and significantly so! The 'over-diluted' solution affected the immune system just as much as the original chemical solution did. Some of the vibrational energy of the allergen must have been imprinted on the water during the dilution process. Professor Benveniste and his team had accidentally proven vibrational medicine.

Amid a degree of controversy, the research was reported in 1988 in the highly prestigious journal *Nature*, stimulating a degree of scientific debate into homoeopathy and, in the eyes of many, lending genuine credibility to homoeopathic medicine, because homoeopathy relies on using very dilute quantities of substances to heal the body. One of the ways in which some homoeopathic medicines work (although not the only way) is by imprinting the vibrational energy of a substance onto a solvent during the succussion process.

Professor Benveniste and his team then went further. Common sense would tell you that if you could reproduce the same vibrations in another way then you could 'fake' a chemical medicine – and that is what they did. In several experiments they recorded the vibrations of some chemical substances onto CD and discovered that by playing the CD they could trigger biological changes to the same degree that they could achieve using the chemical substances.

In one series of experiments they adjusted the amount of blood pumping through a heart according to which CD they played. If, for example, they played the recording of a chemical called acetylcholine, which is known to dilate blood vessels, then more blood would pump through the heart. If they injected a real chemical solution of acetylcholine they got almost identical results. The digitized signal increased blood flow by 21.5 per cent and the chemical solution increased it by 21.3 per cent. It didn't matter to the heart whether it received a chemical substance or just the energy vibrations from the substance.

The team even recorded a set of chemical vibrations and sent them by e-mail from the USA to their laboratory in France, downloaded the signal and played it to an organism. Astonishingly, the signal produced just as many biological changes as a chemical solution. At the time of writing (2006), this research has not been fully embraced by the scientific community but, as is often the case with paradigm-shifting discoveries, I predict that 'digital biology', as it is called, will eventually have a huge impact upon medical science.

If you think about it, a similar thing happens when you play music. All sounds are vibrations and hearing requires vibrations triggering biology in your ear, so all sounds most likely affect your body to some extent, just as Professor Benveniste's CDs do. Hearing classical music, for instance, can alter a person's mood, which involves a movement of neuro-peptides, and might even boost their immune system, smooth the rhythms of their heart and switch sets of genes on and off.

Words and musical sounds are vibrations in space, as are digitized signals, while vibrational medicines are vibrations in water. But a vibration is a vibration – and all vibrations affect us. Some effects are obvious and some are not so obvious.

You probably haven't considered it, but every word you speak, on account of its vibration, affects your body and affects the body of any person hearing it.

Sound and Meaning

Mystics have known and taught for thousands of years that sounds can have profound health-giving effects on the body. Some have said that the sounds 'Ah' and 'O' are primordial sounds, the sounds of creation, and so are found in the name of the creator in just about every culture in the world: God, Jehovah, Yahweh, Ra, to name but a few. In the New Testament, the Gospel of John begins with 'In the beginning was the Word and the Word was with God, and the Word was God.' So, according to John, creation began with the Word – a sound vibration!

A meditation technique known as the Japa meditation involves vocalizing the sound of the creator, whatever that may be to you, over and over again. It is believed to bring you into conscious contact with the creator.

You may have noticed that certain pieces of music affect your mood. Some have a relaxing effect on your body and mind while others have a stimulating effect. Some even give you 'flashbacks' of past experiences, and flashbacks are visualizations, so they probably alter the expression of several sets of genes and alter the patterns of growth in your brain. In fact, you have probably heard of the 'Mozart effect', which popularizes research that listening to Mozart (Sonata for Two Pianos in D major, K.448) can improve mental function.

Research has also shown that music can affect your immune system. A scientific study published in 1996 in the scientific journal *Stress Medicine* showed how certain pieces of music increased levels of the immune system's salivary immunoglobulin A – remember that? One particular piece used in the experiment increased s-IgA levels by 55 per cent.

Earlier we learned that a feeling of appreciation could raise s-IgA levels. The scientists put the two together, asking the test subjects to think 'appreciation' while a specific piece of music was played, and the levels of s-IgA went up by 141 per cent. Quite a therapy!

A study published in 2002 in the journal *Alternative Therapies* showed that group drumming facilitated by a music therapist also boosted the immune system, and even reported that there was a reduction in the levels of some stress hormones with shamanic drumming during the experiment.

Drumming is also used by some shamans to help them enter an altered state of consciousness. The sound vibrations (waves) presumably resonate with some of the body's natural rhythms and cause the production of mind-altering opiate-type neuropeptides that fit into receptors in the emotional areas of the brain. Prolonged drumming probably even involves a number of genes being switched on and off.

In 2005 scientists from the University of Pavia and the University of Oxford found that listening to music affected the heart. When playing selected pieces of music to 24 men and women they found that fast music increased circulation and breathing, and slower, meditative music caused a substantial fall in heart rate.

Similarly, in 2005 a research team led by Dr Shmuel Arnon of the Neonatal Unit at Netanya Hospital in Israel studied the effects of music on premature babies. After playing music for 30 minutes, they found that the babies slept more deeply and had reduced heart rates. In particular, they found that live music (a lullaby, for instance) had the most powerful effect, which should come as no surprise to parents everywhere.

But it is not only music that has this effect. A kind word said to someone can be music to their ears and make them feel comforted, and such a feeling will have a positive effect on their health.

The meaning of your words is clearly important because it triggers thoughts, feelings and mental images. The words 'I love you,' for instance, may mean a lot to a person and make them feel fantastic, and this will have knock-on health-promoting effects. But the actual sound of the words, the vibrations of the vowels and consonants, also affect the body, and this occurs independent of the words' meaning. The sound of the word 'love', for example, contributes to its biological effect just as its meaning does. So words affect us on two levels, through what they mean to us and through the vibrations of their pronunciation. A word, then, is more than a mere description of something, it is a set of vibrations in space. These vibrate at various levels throughout your body. Some may be felt on the skin and some feel as though they go right through you. For instance, have you ever stood beside a loudspeaker in a nightclub? On a deeper level some sounds may resonate with internal organs and, almost certainly, with the chemical bonds between atoms in DNA and in some of the vital proteins and enzymes in your body.

Have you heard of how the human voice can shatter glass? Ella Fitzgerald could shatter a wine glass by holding a specific note. The sound resonated with the internal structure of the glass, eventually causing it to explode into tiny pieces. In a similar way, ultrasound can be used to deliver a knockout blow to kidney stones, shattering them into fragments that can easily be eliminated from the body. In 2006, at Borders General Hospital in Scotland, Dr Paul Syme reported a significant reduction of stroke symptoms using ultrasound.

Could it be possible, then, for human vocal sound to have a positive effect upon serious disease in the human body?

I once watched a video where three doctors from the Huaxia Zhineng Qigong Clinic and Training Centre in Qinhaungdao, China demonstrated this. They stood behind a woman who had a cancerous tumour in her bladder that was approximately three inches wide and a real-time ultrasound scan of the tumour was shown on a screen for the audience to see. Then the doctors began to rapidly chant a sound that means 'Already gone' or 'Already accomplished.' As the audience watched in astonishment, the tumour began to shrink right before their eyes. Amazingly, it disappeared completely in 2 minutes and 42 seconds. The story is recounted in Gregg Braden's excellent book *The Isaiah Effect.*

Researcher Fabien Maman has also studied the effect of sound on cancer. In the early 1980s, he discovered that a series of acoustic notes would destroy cancer cells, leaving healthy ones intact. He also found that a chromatic scale of notes would alter the energy emitted from healthy human cells.

Although some of this work hasn't been fully embraced by mainstream science, it may be just a matter of time before it is. It is often the case that discoveries that are outside our mindsets take time before they become part of the furniture, so to speak.

Maybe there's more truth in the wizardry teachings of Hogwarts than any of us imagine! There might be ancient words, mostly forgotten, that have been used in past times to achieve the most remarkable of things. Who knows? There is much we have to learn and I believe that we are only scratching the surface in understanding how sound affects biology. In fact our understanding of sounds and how they affect matter – biological and non-biological – is still primitive but deserves a great deal of research.

In his book *Power vs Force*, Dr David R. Hawkins uses a technique known as applied kinesiology to determine 'levels of consciousness'. He calibrated a scale between 1 and 1,000, where 1 would represent the consciousness of a bacterium and 1,000 would represent the consciousness of historical figures such as Christ, Krishna and Buddha. He found the average level of consciousness of humanity to be a little above 200, but found that much classical music scored around 500.

It may be that we have an unconscious awareness of the effects of certain pieces of music and other sounds, and just as our beliefs affect our physical bodies, as shown in the placebo effect, so some pieces of music and other sounds may have powerful effects on our bodies. And of course the vibrations of the sound will affect us too.

During 2003 I personally conducted some simple experiments that measured the biological effects of some words. I wrote the words 'love', 'fear', 'happy' and 'sad' on labels and stuck them onto plastic cups. I then put a small amount of water in each of them. By unconsciously triggering tiny levels of emotion in myself, I believed that my awareness of each word would imprint energy associated with its meaning onto the water in each cup.

I then took a set of 30 pots and put approximately 50 seeds of cress in each of them. I then used the 'love'-labelled cup to water six pots of seeds every day and I did the same with 'fear'-labelled cups and the 'happy'- and 'sad'-labelled cups. I also watered a set of six pots with unlabelled water to serve as a control. Each day I put a small amount of water in each cup and used an exact amount of it to water the seeds.

I used six pots for each word so that I could obtain a statistically accurate result – the effect of each word would be measured against 300 'control' seeds. Each set of six pots received water from the same cup every day so that there was no overlap of words on any seeds.

After watering them for seven days I measured the length of every sprout of cress, something I can assure you was no five-minute task.

The results surprised even me. I discovered that the seeds that had been watered from the 'love'-labelled cups grew much taller than the seeds watered from the 'fear'-labelled cups, and the seeds watered with 'happy' water were much taller than the seeds grown with 'sad' water. There was a 7 per cent difference in the height of sprouts between the 'love' and 'fear' cups and a 15 per cent difference between the 'happy' and 'sad' ones (see References). 'Happy' water made the seeds grow tallest of all. And this was after only seven days!

It may be that my awareness of each word, even on an unconscious level, altered the energy output of my body. We know that the electrical output from the heart, for instance, can be measured several inches from the body, and also if you feel, say, embarrassed, people can feel an increase in heat emanating from your face. Some aspects of this energy output may imprint water in such a way that it affects the growth of seeds.

In addition, as outlined later in the book, everything is connected at the quantum level, and so my awareness of the water immediately changed it – the word that I was aware of, as I thought of the water, changed it.

Japanese scientist Masaru Emoto proved that such changes can take place in water by photographing changes in the crystal structure of water brought about by words. A year or two before my experiments he had written down words, stuck them onto bottles of water and used a technique called darkfield microscopy to take photographs of the water after it had been frozen into ice. This clearly showed that different words produced different crystals of ice.

For example, Emoto discovered that the words 'love', 'thank you' and even 'Mother Teresa' produced highly crystalline sparkly ice crystals, but negative words caused crystals to be dull and undefined. He also recorded differences in the structure of water when people had prayed or when different pieces of music had been played in its vicinity. Tibetan or Buddhist chants or pieces of classical music produced sparkly crystals. Emoto has now produced thousands of crystal pictures of water from all over the world. Many of these can be found in his books *Messages from Water*, *The Hidden Messages of Water*, *The True Power of Water* and *Love Thyself*.

This research can be useful to us all every day. I often write inspiring, compassionate, uplifting, peaceful or healing words on labels and stick them onto the bottles of water that I drink from, because I believe that they will nourish my body in some way.

Before eating anything I also quietly say a few words to acknowledge the fact that I appreciate the food that I am about to eat.

Food for the Soul

Most food contains water, so any emotions experienced while preparing it or prior to eating it may colour it. Even if it had no water in it, however, it would still absorb feelings and intentions, given that rocks, which are dry, absorb mental and emotional energy. Scientists use the fact that quartz crystal holds, amplifies and transmits sound and electromagnetic frequencies, which are also vibrations.

In fact it seems as though almost everything can do this. Most psychically sensitive people will tell you that buildings and other places still hold the vibrations, or memories, of past times.

Some interpretations of quantum physics have suggested that thoughts are simply faster vibrations of sound than ultrasound, music or words. We know that to a small degree music will affect the internal structure of any rocks in the vicinity (just as it affects wine glasses), as would ultrasound. So it is logical to assume that thoughts will also be picked up by the internal (quantum) structure of rocks – and other objects – at some level.

So, to go back to food, any thoughts, feelings or words expressed around it will colour it to some extent. Imagine the consequences of eating three meals a day, 365 days a year, after saying a few words of gratitude as you sat down to eat, or even just thinking them. These might be addressed to the creator, however you envisage this, or to the people who provided the food for you. In one year alone that would be 1,095 times where you would have taken positive energy into your body as you ate. It would be an interesting scientific study to compare the health of people who did this with people who didn't, say over the course of a year.

In some cultures, food is carefully prepared with love and gratitude in this way. I find a difference in taste, as well as how I feel afterwards, when I eat food that has been prepared like this.

I attended a talk on food during a meditation retreat in India during 2002, at the invitation of the Brahma Kumaris World Spiritual University, and learned how much importance they paid to where it comes from and the way that it is prepared. At the retreat centre, all food is prepared by people who are mindful of love and is served with a genuine smile and in a spirit of service. I can tell you that the food tasted divine.

There's a lot to be said about taking pride in your cooking. A love of food preparation, cooking and presentation may add more to the quality of the meal than you might imagine.

At one of the lectures in India, the speaker touched on the subject of vegetarian food. He mentioned that meat might be coloured by the way the animal was treated. An inhumane environment and painful death, for instance, would imprint the animal's fear onto the meat. The vibrations of fear would then enter your body as you ate it. If you are going to eat meat, therefore, it might be better to choose meat that comes from animals that have been treated with love and care, or who have roamed free.

This reminded me of something I once heard about some Native American tribes. They would ask the creator to give them food and then, quite frequently, a docile buffalo would wander into their path almost as if it was offering itself up. It was believed that the animal had naturally come to the end of its life and had made an agreement with the creator so it felt no fear or pain when it died. The Native Americans would thank the creator for the gift of food and thank the buffalo for providing nourishment for the people, thereby genuinely honouring its spirit. Such gratitude and compassion would have undoubtedly coloured the meat with love vibrations, nourishing the bodies of all who ate of it.

I am quite certain that if any scientists wish to analyse food before and after such feelings are expressed about it, or before and after grace has been said, then they will discover there to be a significant difference in it.

Saying grace, of course, will also affect any water in the vicinity and the analysis will also show differences in the way its atoms vibrate.

Holy Water

If, say, an apparition appeared near a stream of water then it would colour the water and the surrounding rocks with the energy emitted from it. (It would have to emit energy, which impacts the nerves in the eyes, otherwise it could not be seen.)

Some people may believe that apparitions are merely figments of the imagination, but I will make the assumption that they are real and that some people just can't see them. As quantum physicists have proven, many forms of energy can occupy the same space as we can, it is just that their vibrations are outside the normal range of perception of the human visual cortex. Every person is unique, however, so there may be some with a slightly larger range than others, and these people may be able to see apparitions.

As we have learned, rocks absorb energy, and just as hot rocks slowly give off heat, so they would also radiate the energy of an apparition. And if water were to trickle over the rocks it would be coloured by the energy of the apparition. This might be a reason why 'holy' areas where apparitions have been seen produce healing waters for many years. The healing qualities might last a very long time, because if millions of people knew about it, their faith, beliefs, emotions and intentions would continually infuse it with healing intentions.

The people wouldn't even need to be in the vicinity, given that everything in existence is connected. A number of scientists have studied our ability to send and receive intentions over great distances. It is called 'distant intentional influence', or more commonly 'distant healing'.

6

Distant Healing and Prayer

If a person is in pain or ill, you help them in some way the instant you want them to get better. Every intention goes to where it is intended. And research has shown that it doesn't matter whether you are right beside the person or several miles away. In fact it wouldn't matter if you were on the moon.

Several scientific studies have investigated distant healing, confirming that intention really does affect people over great distances. Typically the experiments had several people in one place visualizing or mentally intending a change to happen in other people at a distance.

In one particular experiment, led by Dr Dean Radin, currently of the Institute of Noetic Sciences in Petaluma, California, but conducted while at the Department of Parapsychology of Edinburgh University, the 'influencers' (the people doing the visualization or sending mental intentions) were asked to try to either calm or activate the other people (the 'targets'). The experiment involved seven 'influencers' and ten 'targets'.

Over 16 individual sessions the influencers were able to influence the targets in a room 25 metres away. The scientists measured changes in the targets using sensors attached to their skin. When asked to either calm or activate the targets, the sensors consistently measured a change when the influencers sent their intentions.

Other research has indicated that if the experiment had been conducted with a few centimetres, or even kilometres, separating the influencers and targets, the results would have been the same. Distance does not count in matters of the mind!

A study involving 96 patients with hypertension reported that influencers could even reduce the blood pressure of targets. The influencers were in one place and targets in another. Blood pressure measurements taken before and after intention was sent showed a reduction in blood pressure.

Professor William Braud and co-workers at the Mind Science Foundation in San Antonio, Texas also studied blood. They showed that intention could slow down the bursting of hypertonic (salty) blood cells even when the influencers and targets were in separate locations.

In a 1998 study reported in the *Western Medical Journal* in the USA, scientists described how distant healing could affect AIDS patients. The study involved 40 patients, with half being given distant healing and half not. After 10 weeks, the scientists found that the patients who had been given distant healing had acquired fewer new AIDS-defining illnesses, had a lower severity of illness, had needed far fewer visits by their doctors and had had fewer hospitalizations and fewer days of hospitalization.

Distant healers can even alter the growth rate of plants. In one experiment, two healers substantially speeded up the growth rate of rye grass when they were 500 kilometres away from it. The grass was monitored as it grew and when the instruction was given for the healers to focus upon it, it immediately started to grow faster. During some periods the rate of growth increased by over 600 per cent.

In a different kind of study, conducted by William Braud and co-workers, several targets were asked to focus their attention on burning candles. Each time their attention slipped they were to press a button alerting the researchers. At this instant, an influencer would focus on the candle and try to mentally assist the targets in their concentration. The results were significant, showing that the influencers had helped the targets to concentrate.

Several studies have also shown that a person is always acutely aware of another person staring at them. You have probably noticed this in your own life. Don't you just get a 'feeling' when someone is staring at you? It's real! Your body is picking up on that person's thoughts on a biological level, and so is your mind. Some people can even physically feel it, which as we already know is probably due to the movement of neuropeptides to specific receptors.

All of these results clearly imply that anyone can have an effect upon the heart, mind and body of anyone else. The effects may be very small, but sometimes they can be large, so this presents all of us with a moral choice.

A significant degree of responsibility is required here. It is morally important to intend no harm towards another. Of course, sometimes it is beneficial to get things out of our systems. Suppressing feelings does no good. But perhaps it is best that we do so with as much tact and compassion as possible. We should endeavour to forgive and to wish the best for each other.

However, if you should feel that others aren't able to wish the best for you, don't despair. Studies have shown that we can easily block unwanted intentions. It can be as simple as declaring: 'Every day in every way I am protected from any harmful thoughts, intentions and emotions of others.'

In one particular scientific experiment involving 32 targets, half were asked to shield themselves from the thoughts of the influencers. It was found that they could easily do so.

Some healing practitioners are well aware that during treatments they pick up their patients' energies – their thoughts, emotions and issues – and that they have to 'psychically protect' themselves. Some therapists like to visualize wearing a 'cloak of protection' made of white or golden light that cancels out any harmful thoughts or emotions coming their way.

In fact there is just as much mental and emotional noise surrounding us throughout the day as there is electrical and magnetic noise. Holding a fluorescent bulb underneath an overhead power line will cause it to light up due to the large electromagnetic field radiating from the cables. In a similar way, people are 'lit up' by the mass fields of thoughts and emotions in densely populated areas.

This is why some meditation teachers suggest that we meditate at sunrise or late at night, and it is also why some spiritual masters live high in the mountains or have done their training in such places. Early in the morning or late at night most people are asleep, so there is less mental noise in the air. In a more peaceful atmosphere, not crowded with mental and emotional noise, it becomes easier to access a deeper state of meditation. For the same reason, I wrote the bulk of this book between the hours of 11 p.m. and 4 a.m.

If you climb high hills or mountains, you may even have noticed that the air is quieter and more peaceful the higher you climb and the further away you get from the mental and emotional noise at ground level.

So, knowing that all emotions and intentions radiate out and have an effect on others, try to be responsible. If someone annoys you or has hurt you in the past, try to let it go and forgive them. Instead of condemning their actions, try to feel some compassion for them. Perhaps they might be in so much inner pain and confusion that they need to act that way. You never know. Instead of seeing a person whose actions you disapprove of, try to see the person underneath who is suffering and to feel compassion for them. If you do this, you won't be putting any harmful 'noise' into the atmosphere.

Practising the art of forgiveness can also be transformational in your own life, enabling you to forget past hurts and move on. For instance, if someone has hurt you in the past, say a past partner, by going over the events in your mind you generate negative emotions, which we know have a negative effect on our bodies. In addition, your focus on the past can prevent you from enjoying a healthy new relationship. Forgiveness helps you to let go and move on with your own life and also improves your mental and emotional wellbeing.

Christ set an example when he said, 'Forgive them, Father, for they know not what they do.'

As well as forgiving others, you can also pray for them. Prayers are very powerful because as well as intention, they bring faith in the creator into play.

Prayer

One of the best-known scientific studies of the power of prayer took place at the University of San Francisco School of Medicine between August 1982 and May 1983. During that time, 393 patients were admitted to the coronary care unit of the hospital and agreed to be involved in the prayer study. It was led by Randolph Byrd, MD, and the results were published in the *Southern Medical Journal* in 1988. Normal medical treatment for all 393 patients took place as required except that approximately half of them were prayed for by a group of Christians who were not in the hospital, and half were not.

The study showed that the overall severity of illness of the patients who were prayed for turned out to be much less than the patients who were not prayed for. The group that was prayed for needed less ventilatory assistance, fewer antibiotics and fewer diuretics than the patients who were not prayed for, and there was also less need for CPR (resuscitation).

Please note that although Christians participated in this study, prayers from any religious group are beneficial. In fact a study took place in 1998 at Duke University Medical Center with 150 patients who underwent heart surgery. Again, half were prayed for and half were not, but this time by different religious groups. It was found that the patients who were prayed for had fewer complications and their recovery rates were 50–100 per cent faster than the patients who were not prayed for.

These controlled scientific studies, and many others, show that prayer really works. And I believe that science is only just scratching the surface of a larger phenomenon that depends on the person or people doing the praying, the person or people receiving the prayer, who outside the study is praying and even the circumstances of the prayer and the people involved in the research. Everything is connected and so every thought counts.

I don't know a single person who hasn't, at some time in their life, called on a higher power to make themselves or someone else well, or even to change something in their life. Prayer works, in my opinion, although you might not always see immediate results or results that you intended.

The reason the result might not be what you asked for is that when you invite God, or whichever deity you pray to, into your life then you are inviting more wisdom and love. Therefore you will get the wisest, most love-filled result that is best for everyone. If your intentions are consistent with that, for example if you desire 'this or something better that will benefit all concerned', then you will probably get what you pray for or something even better. If not, then the results might be different from what you desire, but they will still be the best for everyone concerned.

An interesting phenomenon is that when you genuinely pray for the wellbeing or success of someone else, you also receive wellbeing and success. You get back what you send out.

A scientific study on prayer, reported in 1997 in the journal *Alternative Therapies*, found precisely this. It was led by Fr Seán O'Laoire and investigated the effects of prayer on self-esteem, anxiety and depression. In all, 496 volunteers were involved, 406 as subjects to be prayed for and 90 as agents to do the praying. Three agents prayed for each subject and prayer was offered daily for 15 minutes for an experimental period of 12 weeks.

Evaluations were made at the beginning and end of the study of self-esteem, anxiety, depression, mood, physical health, intellectual health, spiritual health, relationships and creative expression. In all measures the subjects showed improvement but, remarkably, so did the agents, and in some areas – intellectual health, spiritual health, relationships and creative expression – they improved more than the subjects. You get back what you give out!

A 2001 study reported in the *British Medical Journal* also found that the act of praying was beneficial to the person doing the praying. The research studied the effects of rosary prayer and yoga mantras on breathing and on the heart. When the subjects recited *Ave Maria* or a yoga mantra, their breathing generally slowed to six breaths per minute, which is know to oxygenate the blood and be good for the heart. The prayer and mantras also smoothed the rhythms of the heart.

Many people use prayer not only to restore health but also to change aspects of their lives. Ancient Tibetan and Native American teachings, as well as those in the Dead Sea Scrolls, suggest that there are effective ways to pray and ways that are not so effective. Some of these teachings are described in Gregg Braden's book *The Isaiah Effect*.

An effective prayer is one where a person begins with a feeling of genuine gratitude for the current situation. Then they imagine what they desire, either while speaking to a deity or not, and vividly experience their desire being fulfilled. The feeling is key. Lastly, they give thanks for having had the opportunity to choose.

One of the reasons why prayer works, and why visualization and distant healing work, is because everything in the universe is connected to everything else, as we will see in the following chapters.

7

The Nature of Reality

What is reality? If you were to take something and look inside it, you would see the cells that it was made of. Looking even more closely, you would see even smaller organelles floating around in the cells. Looking more closely still, you would see proteins, enzymes and even DNA. And if you were to look inside DNA you would see individual atoms. Going inside the atoms would reveal even smaller parts – subatomic particles. And looking inside them you would find even smaller particles, and then even smaller ones inside them. Eventually you would come to a place with nothing there. Scientists call this the 'quantum field'.

This is the domain of the science of quantum physics. At this level, everything is connected. You are connected to the forests, the flowers, the weeds, the animals, the insects, the fish, the mountains and clouds, even the planets and stars. There are no exceptions. Nothing is left out. No one is alone. Everything that exists was born in the quantum field. Everything condensed out of the field in the same way as, say, raindrops condense out of clouds.

These theories actually parallel those of some Eastern mystical teachings, which also talk of all things condensing out of a field of energy. The only real difference is that Eastern mystics say the field is alive. What we call 'the quantum field' they call 'a field of *qi*' or 'a field of conscious intelligence'.

Some scientists believe that this idea describes reality more accurately than Western scientific theories do, and maybe experiments will eventually confirm this. Even Albert Einstein believed that matter was a point in space where the field was very intense and that the quantum field was the only reality.

At the most basic level, then, everything is composed of consciousness. Therefore, in the human body, at the root (quantum) level, a diseased organ is not an inanimate object but one made of consciousness. This is perhaps why it is possible to heal organs with visualization. It may also be why our genes switch on and off according to how we think and feel. There is an interaction between mind and matter at the quantum level. In other words, consciousness is affecting consciousness, in the same way that steam and water affect ice. Just as steam or hot water can be used to sculpt ice, so thoughts and feelings may sculpt atoms and molecules, restoring health and vitality to any part of the body.

The Collective Unconscious

The famous psychologist Carl Jung proposed the existence of a 'collective unconscious', which is a group unconscious mind that connects everyone together.

According to Jung, each of us has a conscious mind and an unconscious mind. The conscious mind is the day-to-day part of our mind that we think with. We use it for everyday efforts like moving our arms and legs, speaking, smiling, singing and dancing, and to alter our breathing.

The unconscious mind is much larger. Just as you use your conscious mind intentionally to move your body, so the unconscious mind intentionally moves your cells. It also controls your heartbeat, the workings of your hormones and even the production and movement of your neuropeptides. Because it is controlling many more things, it is usually out of reach of our conscious mind. This is why it is called the *un*conscious.

Jung proposed that we all share a collective unconscious mind to which we are connected through our individual unconscious minds. It's a bit like the way computers are connected to the internet. And just as all of us (with the right equipment) can access the internet, so all of us can access the collective unconscious.

Most people imagine that the internet is the network of computers, but it is not. Neither is it the cables or servers. It is the information. The computers are merely devices used to access the information. When a new website is uploaded it changes the internet slightly, not because it affects the computers, but because the total information is now different.

Similarly, the collective unconscious is the total information, or intelligence, of all of us. Whenever new thoughts arise or ideas are generated, it is as if a new website has been posted. It changes the information and intelligence of all of us.

Imagine a room full of people and imagine that they are all holding a single piece of rope so that it connects everyone, like a net. Call it an 'inter-net', or a 'web'. If someone were to shake one strand of the rope, everyone would feel it because they were all connected by it, just as a spider instantly feels the vibrations of something trapped in its web. In this way the entire universe vibrates to the tune of the tiniest thought or idea.

This is the underlying reason why knowledge travels so quickly. It rarely waits until it is read or heard; it is intuitively known by everyone as it vibrates along every strand that connects us. We may learn things through books, newspapers or from the TV, but at an unconscious level we knew them already. These physical devices, whose creation was unconsciously inspired, merely tell us what is already in our unconscious minds. In a way, they also act like the computers that we use to download information from the internet.

We are limited, then, only by our speed of connection. And just as modern advances are providing faster ways of accessing information from the internet, so we are evolving in our level of consciousness and enhancing our abilities to access information from the collective unconscious.

Indeed, looking at the expansion in the number of books published in the mind, body, spirit field in recent times, it would appear that more and more people are expanding their consciousness and so it is likely that our ability to access unconscious information will also improve. And as it does, we will discover faster and faster ways to communicate.

Also, as each new person's consciousness expands, their ideas further vibrate throughout the web, inspiring similar ideas and intuitions in others. Looking at our changing world, I believe that this knowledge is already inspiring us to feel differently and therefore to act differently. And the consequences of our feelings and our actions are profoundly affecting the world.

For instance, we intuitively know that the health of the web, just like a spider's web, is dependent upon every strand.

If one strand is broken, the overall health suffers, even though other strands may appear to be strong. Therefore we are becoming more responsible in our actions, seeking ways of living that are of mutual benefit to all.

It is not always obvious, but there are growing pockets of change occurring everywhere in the world where ways of working together are being created upon principles of kindness, fairness, peace, unity, honesty, connectedness and love. For example, a growing number of businesses with visionary leaders, while retaining their goals of continuous growth, also recognize that they are part of a whole and ensure that their growth benefits that whole. If something is gained at the expense of another, or of any part of nature, then we all lose in the long term.

In his paradigm-shifting book *Birth of the Chaordic Age*, Dee Hock, founder of VISA International, explains how and why some corporations are adapting in this way. He says that within some businesses, the leaders and all of their employees have created a shared moral and ethical sense of purpose and a shared set of principles of conduct concerning how they will treat each other. Common sense will tell you that such corporations and organizations will flourish because everyone shares a similar vision.

Typically, employees of many corporations and organizations don't feel, at a deep level, that they are part of such a moral and ethical vision for the betterment of humanity. However, intuitively, they feel they should be. The knowledge that it is possible is vibrating throughout the web. This is why cracks appear in corporations which still operate by the old rules. In these companies there is often a huge gulf between the goals and behaviour of the company and the inner sense of purpose and behaviour of its employees. So stress and employee dissatisfaction can reach epidemic proportions. The rules are changing, however, because people are changing, because what's in the collective unconscious is changing. The true value and power of a business, or of an individual, is evolving from who *has* the most to who *serves* the most. Watch, over the next few years, and you will be able to see this happening.

Even now, if you look around, you can see more of the changes. For example, investment in ethical businesses is now higher than ever before. There is also a growing desire in the world to respect nature and protect the environment. There is more focus on human rights than ever before in history. More people than ever before are refusing to accept the bullying or abuse of another person. They understand that it doesn't have to be that way. There is also a growing Fairtrade movement, in which a fair price is paid for goods and services, particularly from developing countries.

Charities are also expanding. People from all over the world often race to help their brothers and sisters in need. On 26 December 2004, for example, when a tsunami struck East Asia and caused untold devastation, in a demonstration of global compassion unrivalled in modern times the people of the world rallied together to donate money to help the survivors and to help rebuild the communities that were destroyed. In my own country I read of children giving up their Christmas presents or selling some of their personal belongings. People were donating money over the telephone and the internet and loose change was being collected in cans in numerous shops and businesses. Musicians, sportspeople and entertainers even organized special events in aid of the people affected. Together, we helped repair a deep wound and give others hope in the strength of the human spirit.

The world is becoming a more loving place every day as we grow in consciousness and recognize that we are all members of the same human family.

Our intuitive sense of connection to one another is also reflected in science. In medicine, more and more scientists are beginning to realize that our mental and emotional attitudes are linked with disease and that we can participate in our own healing process and that of others. The number of healthcare practitioners who integrate complementary and allopathic medicine is growing fast.

People are seeing the world differently from the way they did only a few years ago, and their decisions are changing to benefit all of humanity. And as these changes occur they vibrate the web, inspiring similar changes in other people in other parts of the world. We are all affected, because everything is connected.

8

Experiments in Connectedness

Since everything is connected and everything is condensed out of consciousness, it follows that your thoughts can affect *anything*, not just your biology. Each thought, as we know, sends vibrations through the whole web, and so events in your life, and in the world, which are merely a product of the *interaction* of things, are also affected.

Most thoughts produce minor vibrations on the web and these result in minor changes in individual circumstances and in the world. Some scientists have studied this using 'random-event generators' such as computers that constantly print out random numbers. The idea is that such numbers should always be random. That's their nature. If you were to show the randomness on a computer screen you would see a straight line that never changes. However, under certain conditions, it does change.

A 2005 report in the *Journal of Cellular and Molecular Biology* summarized several years of research conducted by the Princeton Engineering Anomalies Research (PEAR) Group at Princeton University. A typical experiment would see a person try to make one number appear more often than any other. And it was possible to do so. An average person, for instance, could make, say, an '8' appear more often than any other number.

Such studies suggest that we interact with reality every moment, although the effects of our thoughts are seldom noticeable unless we are consciously aware of our role in creating our own personal reality. Usually it takes lots of the same kind of thought to have any kind of noticeable effect. Indeed, when a large number of people are focusing upon the same thing at the same time, the changes are more noticeable. However, smaller changes are often observed with just one person and I have confirmed this in my own experiments, recording that my intentions frequently give rise to changes around me.

Each thought sends ripples (waves/vibrations) through the universe, just as dropping a pebble in a pond sends ripples outwards. A single thought produces a small vibration that is hardly noticeable in the world, but millions of the same thoughts cause a big vibration, like the effect of dropping a huge boulder in a pond. Furthermore, each identical wave adds to another, 'resonating' with it and causing a multiplication of its intensity.

Say ten million people heard something on the TV news at the same time and all of them thought, 'Whoa!' That would be ten million people whose minds stopped processing 100 other things and, just for that instant, were focused on the same thing. You would expect this to produce a big vibration. Indeed, numerous experiments have shown that when this type of focusing takes place, a blip appears on the line of the random-event generator. And such is the force of the focusing of millions of thoughts at the same time that the entire web is affected.

Imagine if hundreds or even thousands of people focused on peace at the same time. The thoughts would ripple outwards and the effect could be huge. Experiments have actually shown this.

A paper published in the *Journal of Crime and Justice* in 1981 described the results of some of these experiments. In a typical experiment, several hundred expert meditators gathered together in a city and meditated, using Transcendental Meditation. FBI statistics gathered over the following year recorded substantially lower crime rates. Similar studies have been conducted in several cities around the world.

In other experiments, presented at the American Political Science Association AGM in 1989, around 7,000 meditators successfully reduced recorded incidences of terrorism and international conflict.

So, peaceful thoughts vibrate outwards, affecting the consciousness of people nearby, just as a wave produced by dropping a pebble in a small pond will affect everything floating on the surface of the pond. If millions of people were to focus on peace, then people all over the world might be inspired to behave more peacefully towards each other. With a wave of inspiration travelling through the web, people going about their daily business might just feel different, more relaxed and peaceful. Others might find their problems resolved, since many of our daily difficulties are products of our chaotic minds. Negotiators in conflict situations might suddenly see the solutions to long-running stand-offs. And both sides might suddenly feel less hostile towards each other and even see less meaning in the fighting than they did previously.

All it would take would be for millions of people to focus on peace at the same time on a regular basis. With a 'peace budget' as large as a typical corporate advertising budget, visionary leaders could do a lot of good through the media. Imagine seeing the words 'peace', 'love' or 'happy' 100 or so times throughout your daily newspaper, or hearing those words regularly on the TV news. Or, instead of full-page advertisements selling products, imagine there was an advertisement suggesting that we be kind to each other today. As more people heard about or read about peace, love or happiness on a regular basis, the bigger the wave and the larger the effect.

In 2000, some friends and I founded an organization called Spirit Aid. Our original intention was to organize a special event that would inspire more peace, love and kindness in the world. We hoped that a large mass of people simultaneously focusing upon such values might inspire positive changes all over the world.

The plan was to hold a concert in a large conference centre, which we soon scaled up to a football stadium, and beam it live on TV all over the world. And the key was that in between musical sets we wanted authors and teachers to speak about peace, love and kindness. We hoped that the combination of music and messages might produce miracles. During the organizing phase the nature of the event evolved into a 9-day, 24-event festival of peace in July 2002 that sent waves of peace, love and kindness around the world.

Similarly, on 9 February 2003 the authors and teachers James Twyman, Gregg Braden and Doreen Virtue organized a peace meditation where a few million people around the world 'prayed peace' at exactly the same time, synchronized throughout many different time zones. Shortly after the meditation, there was a veto of the initially proposed UN military action in Iraq.

Individually and collectively, we affect each other and

everything in existence 24 hours a day, 365 days a year. Love inspires more love. Peace inspires more peace. Kindness inspires more kindness. Through both our intentions and actions we change the world. We cannot do anything else. The direction of that change is therefore up to us!

ESP

It is not only random-event generators that show how things are connected. Multi-million dollar particle accelerators demonstrate the connectedness of tiny subatomic particles over large distances. Using these machines, a pair of subatomic particles can be sent at fantastic speeds in opposite directions. One of them is then probed and it can be shown that the other instantly feels it.

Numerous simple ESP (extra-sensory perception) experiments have also shown how everything is connected. In a typical ESP experiment a person has to guess which of a series of cards is being held up. The symbol on the card might be a circle, a square, a triangle or wavy lines. Research has shown beyond any shadow of a doubt that 'guessers' are aware of which card is being held up.

In 1994 a psychologist named Julie Milton, at the University of Edinburgh, collected and summarized the results of 78 individual scientific studies involving ESP guesses by 1,158 ordinary people that had been published in the scientific journals between 1964 and 1993. Her analysis concluded that the odds against achieving the results by chance were over ten million to one. ESP was real.

If you think about these experiments, the person guessing and the person holding up the card are connected, and so also are the person guessing and the card being guessed. The people and the cards are made of the same stuff and are all part of the web. Therefore the identity of the card (its unique type of vibration) is available to the guesser, at least on an unconscious level. All that is required is for the information to be 'downloaded' from the web onto the personal conscious mind of the guesser, just as information is downloaded from the internet onto our personal computers. To someone skilled at downloading, it is just as if the card is being held up in full view. As you might expect, some psychics are adept at it.

If we could learn to tap into the collective unconscious at will, thereby 'improving our download connection speed', we would gain some of its knowledge and wisdom. You would, therefore, expect hypnosis to improve ESP ability because it is known to access the unconscious mind.

In 1994, scientists at the University of New York investigated this. They analysed the results of 25 studies that had been published in scientific journals between 1945 and 1982 and indeed discovered that hypnosis improved people's ability to perform well in ESP studies.

ESP is natural. It is only our belief that it is not possible that obstructs our abilities. It is the same with psychic ability. But anyone can practise ESP or become more psychic. Sometimes in the evening, while I was a university student, I tried to train myself. At first, without practice, I could guess the colour of the next card in a randomly shuffled deck of cards maybe four or five times at best, which is what you would expect. But through practice, which involved learning to recognize my intuition, I was able to score consistently higher, and once, with much meditation practice (almost self-hypnosis), I guessed the colour of the card 11 times in a row and with five of the cards I even guessed the suit. I just had a 'feeling' about each card.

I am no more gifted than anyone else. Anyone can learn to tap into the collective unconscious, just as anyone can learn to connect to the internet. In fact we tap into it all the time.

There is a constant flow of information between the collective unconscious mind and your daily awareness, as you feel every vibration, even though most of the time you are not aware of where specific thoughts, intuitions and impulses come from. In the same way, a leaf floating on the surface of a pond feels the waves created by different pebbles dropped into the pond in various places, but is unaware of the source of each wave.

In our daily lives we are often faced with decisions and frequently make a choice based upon what 'feels right'. It may be that we feel vibrations regarding the probable outcome of each choice, and so we make the choice that we feel is right for us.

Many people believe that angels and spirit guides watch over them and help them with life's challenges. Some native cultures share such beliefs and, according to numerous surveys, so does a very large portion of Western culture. When I give talks, a quick show of hands often reveals that over 90 per cent of the audience share these beliefs.

If you assume that angels and spirit guides exist then they too must be part of the web, since nothing can be separate from it. But in a universe with consciousness as its most basic building block it is quite likely that intelligence takes forms other than human. Therefore it seems quite probable that other intelligent entities could download information to us concerning the best course of action to take. Many people claim to have been so inspired.

I myself had an amazing experience in late 2002. I had created a website for Spirit Aid but then had moved on to other things. My late friend Pat was taking over responsibility for the website and asked if I could give her a disc with the website on it. I didn't have any CDs to save it onto, so I went to the shops to buy some. When I was there I noticed several packs of floppy discs and I felt a sudden impulse to buy them and save the website onto floppy discs instead of CDs. But I ignored the feeling and bought a pack of CDs because they had larger storage capacity.

When I arrived home I opened up the website files on my computer, put a CD in the CD drive and pressed 'save'. But it didn't work. I tried again and again, but I couldn't get the website to save onto the CD. I tried every CD in the pack but had no success and began to assume that they were damaged in some way.

I had agreed to hand the website to Pat the next morning, so I was beginning to feel a wee bit concerned that I wouldn't have it ready on time. Knowing that such a mindset wouldn't help, I got up and decided to leave it until later, when I might feel more relaxed.

Since it was a nice day, my partner Elizabeth and I went for a drive. We had no idea where we wanted to go, so just kept on driving. Each time we passed an exit from the motorway we wondered if we should take it, but always decided that we should drive on. Turning off the motorway at those times didn't feel right. Eventually I picked up the map to see if I felt inspired to visit any place in particular. I noticed a small village on the river Forth that I had never heard of before and suggested that we go there.

After driving for almost an hour, we pulled into an empty car park on the outskirts of the village. It was like a ghost town and I quite expected to see tumbleweeds roll past. But as we pulled up to park our car, our attention was drawn to something odd. There was a small box lying on the ground in one of the empty parking spaces. I looked at it and, shocked, realized that it was a box of floppy discs. I couldn't believe it. We were in the middle of nowhere, tumbleweeds (almost) rolling by, in an empty car park, in a place that we had picked at random, and there was a box of floppy discs.

I decided not to touch them in case someone had dropped them and was now on their way back to collect them. Judging by the lack of life anywhere, this was unlikely. But we left them alone anyway.

We walked around the village, had some lunch and returned a couple of hours later, only to discover that the discs were still there. In a way, this was not surprising, as we had only seen about half a dozen people all day, including the two who worked in the café where we had had lunch. But by now I was getting the message. Those discs were meant for me, so I took them.

When we got home, after dinner I decided to have another go at saving the website onto CD. I made several attempts and then the penny finally dropped. I was trying to save a file onto a CD when I didn't even have a CD-writer! I was trying to do it from the normal CD-ROM drive (I had an old computer).

For the previous six months, among my other responsibilities I had been the designated IT person in the charity office and had encountered about every conceivable computer problem and software usage that you can imagine. Yet I hadn't even realized that I needed a CD-writer to save files onto CD. I had needed floppy discs all along.

It was a very large website and as I was saving the files the computer kept telling me that each disc had become full. When the website was finally saved it had taken all ten floppy discs from the box, with absolutely no space left over at the end. I just looked up and said, 'Thanks!'

So, coming back to ESP, people receive information from the collective unconscious all the time, because it is not possible to disconnect from it. It seems that the more relaxed and mentally uncluttered we are, the clearer the information we receive. The technique I used in my personal ESP experiments first helped me to relax, clearing some of the mental noise that often obstructs connection. But it also helped me to overcome some residual beliefs that I held at the time that ESP wasn't possible and so caused me to have more faith that it was possible. And this, I discovered after several more experiments, was the key to my ability. My belief made it easier for me to access information. Faith, I discovered, meant the difference between broadband and dial-up.

Conversely, a belief that it is not possible to connect seems to obstruct the connection and therefore the flow of information from the unconscious to the conscious. This is why people who are sceptical don't get good results.

A lot of people are sceptical as to whether anything out of their mindset is possible, and you have probably heard them say, 'I'll believe it when I see it.' But people who have accomplished great things in life will testify to it being the other way around. Ability follows belief. As Dr Wayne Dyer aptly titled one of his books, *You'll See It When You Believe It*.

Sheep and Goats

In 1993 a psychologist named Tony Lawrence at the University of Edinburgh gathered together the results of 685,000 ESP guesses by 4,500 people performed over a 50-year period from 1943 to 1993. They were called 'sheep-goat experiments'. A 'sheep-goat experiment' is one that compares the ESP ability of people who believe that ESP is possible with that of people who do not.

Lawrence's analysis of the experiments showed that believers ('sheep') were much better at ESP than non-believers ('goats') and the odds against achieving such results by chance were a staggering one trillion to 1.

This confirms that people who believe in ESP are better at ESP than people who don't. So the placebo effect extends much further than taking empty pills. People who don't believe in ESP obstruct their own connection, while people who are open to believe that everything is connected give themselves the ability to gain great wisdom and understanding of life through enhancing their connection. One of the by-products I have noticed is that they also tend to find meaning in their own lives and begin to recognize the contribution that their presence makes to the world.

Belief is a powerful thing. Imagine we believed that the world was a good place, populated by billions of kind and compassionate people. If we did that, we might collectively inspire more kindness and compassion in the world through the waves we created. In fact, as more of us begin to see the world in this way, focusing upon the goodness, our thoughts resonate with each other and multiply the power of the wave.

In the same way a cynical view, focusing instead upon the smaller numbers of people who sometimes act differently, might inspire unhappiness. But whatever happens can be viewed as positive or negative. It's how you choose to look at it that determines what you get out of it. We don't all need to try to change the world. All we really need to do is change our minds *about* the world. If we view the world as a beautiful place, with beautiful people, and if we are willing to believe in the beauty that we see, then our faith will move mountains!

9
Who am I?

For millennia mystical teachings have told us that consciousness condenses to form the physical world, just as steam condenses to form water and ice. In the last century a similar idea has been embraced by a number of scientists. Indeed, there are some parallels between mystical teachings, which are based upon spiritual experience, and modern science, which is based upon intuition and reasoning.

Some mystical teachings tell us that one consciousness is the building block, or source, of the universe and that it is infinitely intelligent. This consciousness is often referred to as 'God' (or the equivalent in other spiritual and religious traditions) and thus everything is part of God. In quantum physics, it is believed that all matter comes from the quantum field and that everything is an expression of the field.

Mystics hold that all matter condenses from the field of infinite intelligence and quantum physics holds that all matter appears at points where the quantum field is most intense.

Since we are conscious beings, I believe that an accurate description of reality must include consciousness, therefore I resonate more with the mystical teachings, although I also embrace the theories of quantum physics, since both seem to look at the same thing in different ways.

Spiritual Amnesia

If all things have their source in the field of infinite intelligence, it may be assumed that there are no accidents and that every form appears and performs exactly as it should. So we are all perfect, all part of the whole. But somehow in the process of condensation we lose the awareness of our true nature. It is like a droplet condensing out of an ocean of conscious intelligence and in noticing that it has become a droplet forgetting that it was once, and is still, part of the ocean.

We thus learn to define ourselves purely in terms of our physical form. You might liken it to an iceberg floating upon the surface of the ocean. Our conscious awareness represents the tip of the iceberg, but the greater part of us – call it 'the Higher Self' – is beneath the surface. And since all we see is the tip of the iceberg, we assume that our consciousness is merely part of our physical selves – the product of the interaction of different chemicals in the brain.

Some teachers hold that our purpose in life is to regain full awareness of our true nature, a state called enlightenment. Each situation in life provides us with an opportunity to do this. Our experiences also reflect our degree of enlightenment, or level of consciousness, as it's often called. An unenlightened person might see the loss of a personal possession, for instance, precisely as a loss and might even assume that it is the result of theft, but an enlightened person might see the same situation as part of a cosmic energy pattern unfolding and experience it as a blessing. Life, then, is a journey of experiences leading us to enlightenment. We are walking a path towards realizing that we *are* the infinite intelligence, though suffering from a little amnesia.

This temporary state of amnesia is why we appear to lack the ability to heal ourselves of any illness or to make positive changes in our lives. We do not lack this ability. It is probably even 'encoded' in our DNA as sets of genes. But we believe we are limited, and so we perform in accordance with the limits we believe in.

At present, 'healing' or 'transformational' genes undoubtedly exist but are switched off in most people. But it is likely that such genes merely await our genuine recognition of who we really are, at which time they may switch on.

Even now, we are personally creating our bodies every day. Old cells die all the time and new ones are born. In this way, your entire body is constantly being renewed under your direction.

Clearly this is not conscious. The part that is doing this is the main body of the iceberg – the Higher Self. Therefore, your Higher Self intended to create your body just the way it is. And the intention to create it, and how it should look and work, would have produced ripples throughout the web. It may have condensed as sets of genes in your DNA. So DNA might be much more than an inherited genetic code. It probably encodes the intention of the Higher Self. And, as genes are expressed through life, that intention materializes as the physical body.

We know, however, that we influence some of our genes through our daily thoughts, so we are never stuck with the decision our Higher Self once made for us. We have the freedom to make any changes that we choose to make, in accordance with what we believe is possible, of course. Our intentions can be very powerful – they even affect the creation of matter.

Creating Reality

Intentions can influence the creation process in two ways. On the one hand, they produce neuropeptides, as we learned in Chapter 2, which circulate around the body and fit into receptors, where they bring about changes, including switching genes on and off. But at a deeper level, they influence the point at which consciousness condenses into subatomic particles.

Think of it like painting a picture. On one level the paint mixes to produce the colours that give the image of, say, a tree, but at a deeper level you imagined the tree in your mind and directed the brush. The end result is the same.

In life, say you wanted to visualize the healing of a damaged organ. The organ, like the entire body, is constantly being regenerated. When you make new healthy images through visualization, your thoughts and feelings produce neuropeptides that switch some internal processes on and off, so that your body begins to evolve into the picture you visualized. And on the deeper level, your intentions influence the creation process, sending pictures to the place and moment when vibrations become particles and so influencing the nature of the particles.

In these ways, many new cells are born according to the healthy images (the blueprint) you modelled them on. The more you visualize new healthy cells, the more new healthy cells are created. This is why visualization is known to have produced miracles.

Where a damaged organ remains damaged for several weeks, new cells will have completely replaced old ones, yet the new ones will have adopted a damaged state. Why? Perhaps because you believed the organ was damaged. This belief, and the mental images and feelings associated with it, influenced the creation of new cells so that they became perfect copies of the old ones.

No one wants to maintain an illness, of course, but it is not easy to switch off a belief in it. Such beliefs are very powerful because illness is a daily reality for many people and therefore is a very deeply ingrained worldwide belief. To create healing miracles requires the ability to overturn, or transcend, this belief. There are very few people on the planet who have been able to do this, but that doesn't mean that we can't all do it. We all have the capacity to overturn beliefs in disease and to form healthy beliefs, just as we can get around a belief that we can't, say, jump over a rock on a path and then jump over it. In the end, the stronger belief wins. If a belief in health is stronger than a belief in illness then the illness will disappear, and vice versa.

And just as conditions in our bodies respond to our thoughts and feelings, so our lives usually quite accurately reflect the state of our minds. In this way we actually create our own reality. First, our intentions open us to receive intuitions that guide some of the things that we think, say, do and even notice around us. And secondly, our thoughts and emotions send out signals, which we know vibrate the web, so they register in people's minds (unconsciously) and in their bodies. Then what happens is that people who happen to have the knowledge, connections and resources to make our thoughts real are unconsciously attracted to us.

This is great if your thoughts are focused on the things you want, but have you ever noticed that when you hurry to reach a place at a specific time, obstacles almost always appear in your path? If you are driving, you can bet that a slow driver will be ahead of you or others will cut in front of you. You might even end up in a traffic jam. Slow drivers will unconsciously gravitate towards you, just so they can answer your unconscious 'I am late' call and so help you to fulfil it.

I remember once when I was running very late for an appointment. I was hurrying and began to notice a series of obstacles appearing as I drove. Most of us, when such obstacles arise, hurry even more, but this just creates more obstacles. Then we start to curse the obstacles. Believe me, I have done this on more than one occasion. However, after years of repeating the same thing I began to realize that what was required at such times was the opposite.

On this occasion, instead of hurrying even more, I chose to pull over and spend a few moments relaxing. While hurrying I was reinforcing a belief that said, 'I am late.' By pulling over, a new belief was forming in my mind. Even though I was consciously aware of my lateness, my actions were contradicting this and thus removing the foundations of the belief. A new unconscious belief was beginning to form, as a result of my pulling over, that said, 'I have plenty of time.' Unconscious beliefs often form according to our actions. Now I would be sending out different unconscious signals and attracting different drivers around me.

After about five minutes of relaxation I started up the car again and peacefully drove to my destination obstacle-free. When I arrived, it turned out that my hostess was also running late and my 'lateness' had, thankfully, given her more time to get ready. It's funny how things work out!

By changing my actions and my belief I changed what was happening. That was a simple example, but if you remember that reality mirrors your thinking, changing any area of your life is well within your control and you need never be at the mercy of any person, organization or situation. Change your mind – your thoughts, your emotions and beliefs – and you will change your life.

Life Changes

Visualizing how you want things to be is a good way to change something and huge numbers of people have found this to be successful. This is where, for instance, you clearly imagine what you want, perhaps even writing it down or drawing a picture of it. Your focus on it then begins to alter things around you, attracting the right people to you and giving you intuitions that guide what you see and where you go, so that what you focus on begins to unfold around you.

I have noticed, though, that while most people have a lot of success in making life changes this way, for some people things eventually revert back to the way they were before. This is because while visualization and intentions are powerful enough to make obvious changes, your old beliefs often reassert themselves. As they do, negative things just 'seem to happen' and you end up in the same situation as before.

For instance, say you find yourself in a job you don't like and you long for something better. You might start to visualize your 'new job' and quite soon, as if by magic, you might get an interview and be offered a job that turns out to be very close to what you imagined. This is natural and simply demonstrates the way that thoughts become reality.

For a few weeks everything might be great in your life but then changes might begin to occur in your new workplace. People might move on and new people might join. Internal systems and practices might change. You might start to have disagreements with some of your new workmates. Before long you might find yourself in a similar situation to the one you left.

This is usually because while you were in the old job you built up a few unconscious beliefs such as 'I don't deserve a meaningful job' or 'I can't get a good job' or 'It's not possible to be in a meaningful job' or 'People at work are not nice.' These beliefs built up because you interpreted what happened to you, often unconsciously, in one of these ways. For example, if you had little or no success in getting a new job, despite sending out a large number of applications, you might build up the belief that you couldn't get a good job. Powerful beliefs like this will begin to build a reality that ensures that your experience remains 'according to your beliefs'.

This has happened to me on a number of occasions, but I have found that there are ways to make lasting changes.

The first requires courage. It is to take such big actions that there can be no turning back. That way, there is little possibility of your old beliefs recreating a similar situation because things have changed so much that it is almost impossible to hold the same beliefs that you did before. For example, the belief that you are stuck in a job you hate will certainly change if you resign.

The second is more subtle but immensely powerful, and it is to examine your attitudes and beliefs about yourself, your life and the world.

One way to do this is to write down how you feel. Cover several pages if you need to, listing all your grievances, annoyances, judgements and frustrations. But do so with the thought that somewhere in all this there is a belief (or a few beliefs) that is causing things to be the way they are and you intend to discover it.

Once you have identified the root belief, change it by writing down its opposite. Then repeat the new belief to yourself several times over the next few days or weeks. Then visualize what you choose to have in your life. You will now often find that when things do change, the change is lasting.

The power of belief is immense. We know how powerful the placebo effect is in creating health. But a similar type of placebo effect happens in our daily lives. Our thoughts, intentions, feelings and beliefs all create what happens to us.

'Feelingization'

Looking at the placebo effect, I recognize that feelings carry great power. If a person with a headache takes a placebo, believing it to be a painkiller, it is not only their belief in the medicine that is a healing factor but also their expectancy that they will get better and their feeling that something positive will happen. Similarly, when a person feels moved to tears, it is not so much the event but the feelings *produced* that have the biological consequences.

On a deeper level, the creation of proteins in the body can be the product of feelings during the memory-storage process. Scientific studies have suggested, as we learned in Chapter 3, that strong feelings accompanying an experience will ensure that it is encoded strongly as brain cells. Each mental and emotional replay of the event re-expresses the genes that manufacture the proteins in the brain. It is the intensity of feeling that leads to the re-expression of the genes.

In a real sense, then, feelings accelerate the creation of matter. They influence the condensation process. So perhaps the best way to visualize good health is to generate a *feeling* of what it might be like to be in good health and the type of things you would do in good health. Similarly, the best way to create life changes is to generate a feeling of what the new reality would be like. I call this 'feelingization' instead of 'visualization', to emphasize the need to feel. The mental image merely gives direction to the feeling.

Using the new job analogy, you might then imagine yourself in the new job (as if it is actually happening) while vividly feeling what it would be like. Try to generate states like excitement, fascination, wonder, awe, joy, laughter and enthusiasm, as these are powerful states. The feeling carries the creative power and accelerates the creation of what you want. It sends a stronger wave throughout the web than a thought does – making your 'unconscious call' louder, so to speak.

You might imagine, for instance, the type of job and location, and even how close or far away it is from home, while joyfully thinking, 'This is so great.' You might imagine new people with the types of personalities that you resonate best with and get excited as you imagine yourself having the types of conversations you love to have.

Any thoughts, then, which carry a strong emotional charge will quickly materialize and those without any feeling will take longer to become reality. This means both positive and negative thoughts. However, any negative experience created in this way can be just as quickly neutralized with a surge of positive thought and emotion.

All thoughts can be amplified by the power of feeling or belief – faith. When you have a lot of faith, or strong positive feelings about a new situation, healing in the body or life changes can be instantaneous. This is why the placebo effect heals. When you believe (feel certain) you will recover instantly, then you do. When you believe (feel certain) it will take time, then it takes time. Feeling and faith are much more than 'mind over matter'. It is really a case of 'mind creates matter'.

Changing the World

When you fully move beyond your amnesia, creation can be instantaneous. From this higher state of consciousness you no longer just believe that you create your body and your life, you *know* – which is a feeling of total certainty.

Spiritual teachings tell us that it is possible for us to grow enough in our consciousness to gain some of the awareness and knowledge of the Higher Self. At such a level of consciousness, beliefs – and so feelings of certainty – about what is possible are intense.

Indeed, Christ said:

'I tell you the truth, if anyone says to this mountain, "Go, throw yourself into the sea," and does not doubt in his heart but believes that what he says will happen, it will be done for him. Therefore I tell you, whatever you ask for in prayer, believe that you have received it, and it will be yours.'

Mark 11:22–4

You will be aware that Christ and Krishna could materialize solid objects out of thin air, turn water into wine and perform instant healing. At their level of consciousness, they could consciously condense vibrations into particles, commanding the formation of atoms and molecules out of thin air. They lived as if they were Higher Selves.

Yogis and mystics also have a degree of conscious control over the creation process as a result of years of meditation and practising exercises that can develop consciousness. This is why they are able to perform many miraculous feats.

Such feats are becoming increasingly possible because the knowledge of our true nature is vibrating through the web, inspiring more and more people. In my own life, I have observed this more and more with each passing year. Additionally, people whom you might never have imagined would do so are now thinking about spiritual connections, the effects of thoughts and emotions on the body, and even angels, and embracing such ideas as if they had thought that way all their life. I have spoken with people from different parts of the world who agree that the same is happening where they live too.

Collectively, our attitudes and behaviour are changing and so we are changing the world. All of us send thoughts, intentions and feelings along the strands of the web. And just as our personal thoughts influence biological events in our bodies and the events of our lives, so our collective thoughts generate tidal waves that influence world events.

So, as we are evolving in our consciousness, moving beyond our temporary state of amnesia, we are changing the world. It is becoming more beautiful every day because we are making it so. At times it may not appear to be so, but events that are not obvious examples of love are simply 'healing in progress'. Sometimes to jump high you need to dip first to generate the momentum. Perhaps the same happens in our lives and in the world at large.

What is being revealed everywhere as we evolve in our consciousness is that our natural state is love.

Love

Love is the force behind all intention. It was behind the intention of the Higher Self to create your body and it was behind God's intention to form the entire universe. If blowing on still water is the creative force that makes waves on water, then love is the substance of the wind that forms the waves.

That is why it is said that God (or the equivalent in other spiritual and religious traditions) breathed life into the universe. All of the universe was created, with love, out of thin air and ultimately has God as the intelligence behind its shape and its action. And as you are ultimately that intelligence, even though you might not yet be conscious of it, you are the guiding intelligence behind all things. What a responsibility!

It has been said that if you act wealthy, you will become wealthy; if you act poor, you will become poor. If, when faced with challenging situations, you consistently ask yourself, 'What would God do now?' and act according to the answer you get, then you will evolve in your consciousness and will make a more consciously positive difference in the world.

Every action you take in life is ultimately motivated by love, even though experiences often cloud our judgement, leading us to act in ways that appear quite far removed from love. This state, the absence of love, is the state of total amnesia called fear.

Love and fear are the roots of all experience.

10
Love, Fear and Biology

Love has a powerful effect on the body, naturally, because it is the force behind its creation. Common sense would therefore tell you that a heart and mind full of love would give you more success in healing yourself, others, your plants, your pets, your life and even the world.

A scientific study at Ohio State University of Medicine was examining the effects of a high-fat and high-cholesterol diet on rabbits. Scientists were feeding them the diet for a period of time then examining them for evidence of atherosclerosis. The atherosclerosis level was expected to be very high throughout the rabbits but one group had 60 per cent less of it than the other groups. Eventually it was discovered that one of the technicians had taken this group out of their cages every day and stroked them.

A repeat of the experiment confirmed this. The loving act of care and compassion had reduced levels of atherosclerosis by 60 per cent. It had altered the biology of the rabbits enough to give them some protection from the damaging effects of a high-fat and high-cholesterol diet.

This came as a surprise to the researchers, but, as we now know, a mother's touch will switch on genes that produce growth hormones, and love also helps the growth of children. So the feeling of love aids the biology-building process and causes an increase in gene expression that offers protection against disease.

Love is also important in successful prayer. When you pray for someone's health or wellbeing, a good prayer contains a feeling of care and compassion for the person you pray for. And God, or whatever deity you pray to, is unconditionally loving, so the love is coming from two directions.

Love is important in all forms of healing. People who practise healing techniques know that the starting point is always care, compassion and a genuine willingness to help.

In the example of the cacti giving up their thorns, love and tenderness were key. There is real truth in the 'old wives' tale' that talking to your plants makes them grow better, especially when you speak kindly to them. In my own plant research described earlier, the words 'love' and 'happy' caused cress seeds to grow much more quickly than normal. Seeds, like all life, thrive in a positive and loving environment.

You can easily conduct your own simple experiments to confirm this by measuring the growth of your plants over a couple of weeks, either with a ruler or by taking photographs. Talk to them kindly every day and you will find that they will respond, just as people do. They will grow taller and stronger and be healthier.

Fear, as you would expect, has the opposite effect on biology. In my own research, the words 'fear' and 'sad' suppressed the growth of the seeds of cress. You may also have noticed that plants do not generally grow as well in negative or depressive environments.

Consistent anger and frustration, both qualities of fear, can suppress the immune system and make heart rhythms shaky. Appreciation, care and compassion do the opposite.

We also know that sustained neglect of an infant, which probably leaves it feeling alone and fearful, suppresses specific genes so much that its growth is hampered. Fear is detrimental to health, whereas love is beneficial.

In general, love promotes health and growth of mind, body and spirit, whereas fear has the opposite effect.

Love and Intention

As already mentioned, any form of healing starts with love. Healing means to 'make whole' and love always seeks to make whole.

In some distant-healing plant-growth experiments, love was the ingredient that was needed to make the plants grow. Some of the healers involved said that they could not bring about any significant changes until they had made a caring and compassionate connection with the plants.

An experiment by Glen Rein of Quantum Biology Research Labs in New York and Rollin McCraty of the Institute of Heartmath showed that love even allowed people to mentally influence the behaviour of DNA. Research into gene expression has shown that genes are switched on and off depending on how you are thinking or feeling, but there is no direct intention in those experiments such as 'I am visualizing switching on such-and-such a gene now' (although this should be possible and could easily be measured). However, the Rein and McCraty experiment showed that the feeling of love could make DNA directly respond to intention.

In the experiment, a group of people were given a jar containing DNA and were asked to try to mentally unwind the two strands while the scientists followed the behaviour of the DNA using spectroscopic techniques. Half of the group had been instructed in standard Heartmath techniques for generating a genuine feeling of love and appreciation and half had not.

Only the people who felt love and appreciation were able to unwind the strands of DNA. The efforts of the other group had no effect. The feeling of love was vital in being able to mentally influence DNA.

This shows that, at a very deep level, healing with intention is much more likely to occur when you have a genuine wish to help.

It follows that if you show kindness, care and compassion to everyone around you – family members, friends, colleagues and people you come into contact with – you will have a beneficial effect on them and on yourself. What you give out always comes back in one form or another. The love you give out will affect your own body and your life.

Love is inside you, even if you don't always see it. Let it out! Kindness can be a simple smile, or a few choice words, or agreeing to help someone. Care and compassion can be listening to someone who needs to talk or even just appreciating the differences in people.

Love can be active. Share it out a bit and you will notice that others will do the same. Your words and actions will unconsciously give people permission to rise to new heights. That can be your gift to them.

11

Mass Reality

In the same way that we participate in the creation of our bodies and the reality of our lives, so we influence the whole world and all of the events that happen in it. Our Higher Selves manufacture the atoms and molecules, but our collective daily thoughts and feelings influence the process.

Have you ever seen a cartoon where a depressed person has a black cloud over their head? If you feel consistently depressed then there will be a depressed mental and emotional atmosphere around you, just like a black cloud. And people sense it. Similarly, if you are happy and joyful, you will be surrounded by a joyful atmosphere and this will also be quite apparent to people who come into contact with you. Indeed, our emotional atmospheres are infectious and interact as we mix with each other.

With a population of over six billion people on the planet, there is a lot of mixing and merging going on. So a collective mental and emotional climate surrounds the world, representing the sum total of six billion or so individual mental and emotional climates.

Have you ever seen a satellite picture of the Earth from space? There are swirls of cloud, some storm fronts and some large areas of clear sky. A similar picture can be drawn for the collective mental and emotional climate. In some areas the climate might be joyful and in others it might be unhappy. These areas might be entire continents or they might be small areas such as a household, an office or a building.

Of course within each of these areas there will be a spread of different mental and emotional climates corresponding to the differences in the people there. For instance, say the mental and emotional climate for a group or area was at level 7 out of 10, this would not mean that everyone living there was at level 7. There would be people at level 3 and 9 too, but taken collectively, the climate would average out at 7.

We tend to gravitate towards people and places that resonate with us. You might have noticed in your own life that there are places where you feel better or worse than usual – perhaps more positive or more peaceful, or more anxious or agitated. Wherever you go you are affected by the mental and emotional climate of the area.

So in the same way that our unconscious minds are linked to form a collective unconscious mind, our conscious mental and emotional states form a collective mental and emotional climate state. And just as our personal thoughts and emotions influence the biological events in our bodies and the daily events in our lives, so the collective thinking of a small or large group influences local or large-scale events.

Group Consciousness and Group Health

Group consciousness is the collective consciousness of any group

– a family, village, town, city, nation, continent or species – and plays a role in why some places can experience positive or negative states of health. Just as a disease in the body can be a consequence of mental stress, so an illness (like a cold, for example) in a family group can be sustained through collective patterns of thinking and feeling within the group.

Of course this can also be easily explained by considering the food we eat, our lifestyles and, in the case of disease, the physical spreading of viruses through contact or through the air. There are many causes of illness, but remember that consciousness precedes biology. It condenses to form it. It is not the other way around.

A friend recounted a funny story to me. He was on an aeroplane and his attention was drawn to a woman at the back of the plane shouting, 'I'm going to be sick!' as she hurried towards the toilets at the front. He was having 'one of those days' and he shook his head and thought to himself, 'I bet she stops right at me and throws up.' You know what? She passed dozens of people, stopped right at him, turned to face him and threw up over him.

You may have noticed that sometimes we do attract situations like magnets. Our thoughts, feelings, beliefs and issues send a pulse through the web, causing people to bring us exactly what is appropriate to our current state of mind. And a disease-carrying insect or an airborne pathogen will respond just as well as a person will.

Of course, this does not mean that all diseases and events are the direct product of conscious thoughts and feelings. It is very clear that a vast number of people infected with, say, HIV and AIDS did not attract the disease through their thinking. In terms of mass disease there must be a deeper spiritual significance as to why a person is born into those conditions, a purpose known only to the Higher Self. Some hope may lie in the fact that a change of mind can cure disease in an individual, therefore a change of mind in a nation, through education perhaps, could save many lives.

Transcending group consciousness is not easy. Individuals with different attitudes and beliefs usually begin to adopt a similar mindset to the rest of the group. In the same way, though, many people educated to a new mindset will influence others in the group. A mindset of health will eventually eradicate a disease, partly through altering conditions inside the body, partly through inspiring individuals to act differently and change their habits, and also through unconsciously inspiring people in different parts of the world to find cures or provide aid. The bottom line is that eventually the stronger mindset wins!

Changing the World

In general, events are more likely to occur in areas where the mental and emotional climate resonates with them. Areas where conflict has been regular throughout history are more likely to experience fighting, for example, than regions where this has not been the case. People in such areas have known conflict, so the idea is strong in the group consciousness and will inspire individuals to resolve their differences that way.

Changing the nature of events requires changing the group mind. History has taught us that this will most likely start with one person or a small group of individuals or even because of the introduction of new people to the group.

To reiterate, with some events – natural disasters and epidemics among them – there is no apparent link between the mental and emotional climate of an area and an event. However, all must have a spiritual source, known to the Higher Self of everyone affected, which we may or may not ever understand at a conscious level.

It is possible that a natural disaster on a very large scale, for instance, might happen so that we can grow from it and learn compassion. In the grander scheme of things, then, such events are created to move the world closer to enlightenment – to a higher level of consciousness. The Higher Selves of the individuals who lose their lives would have chosen to be part of the event and at some level each person would have been aware of this. There can be no accidents in our conscious universe.

Essentially, our collective Higher Selves bring everything into materialization and our collective mental and emotional state influences the process. It shapes the energy vibrations and particles on a global level, organizing them into a format that accurately reflects, as events, the average state of consciousness of humanity. And on the surface, our collective thoughts and feelings vibrate the web and inspire individuals and groups to act in such a way that the world reflects our state of consciousness. We get what we concentrate upon in our own lives and we also get what we concentrate upon in the world. A world of peace and joy reflects an overall inner climate of peace and joy, and a world where conflict is rife represents a significant degree of personal unrest and unhappiness.

Of course, this does not mean that everyone has the same influence over every event. Some people have a larger effect than others. If the average mental and emotional climate is 5 out of 10, people who are 8s and 9s, for instance, might have more of a sustaining effect on positive events, while people who are 2s and 3s might have more of an effect on situations of conflict.

But if you wish to change anything, start with yourself. Examine the contents of your own mind, *honestly*, and notice what you are feeding into the collective mental and emotional climate. Is there a conflict in your life that you are actively participating in? Or even in your mind? If you know of a conflict, whether in your family group, your work environment or an entire nation, notice if you judge the people involved. Do you condemn their actions? If so, then you merely feed the conflict. Think about it! Perhaps your contribution is not as great as that of the people directly participating, but you are still playing a role.

Therefore, make any changes to your own attitudes and behaviour that you believe are required until what you project outwards is consistent with what you wish to see in the world. You will very quickly notice that the type of events in your life will change, and gradually the nature of world events will change too, but it all begins with you.

You could even help others to change their mental and emotional climates, and then you will have a greater effect on the world. This is why the peace prayers described earlier, and others like them, influence world events. As more and more people join together, they have a greater effect. The group intentions project outwards, sending large waves along the web that have a large effect upon the global mental and emotional climate, and this then shapes events in the world.

If many of us try to see the best in each other, forgiving where it is necessary, acting peacefully, joyfully and kindly towards each other, then forgiveness, peace, joy and kindness will colour the mental and emotional atmosphere of the world and will be introduced into the world.

If enough of us want to help those in need and act on our desire with gestures as simple as flashing a genuine smile, saying something nice, making a donation, helping an elderly person with their shopping, allowing a car in front of us in a traffic jam or even inviting someone to go in front of us in the supermarket queue, then we will find that more assistance will reach people on a global scale. Those who need help might be thousands of miles away, but our intentions will vibrate the web and inspire those who are in the right place and have the necessary resources to offer help where it is needed.

It's all down to us, with every breath we take, every thought we think. Each of us is far more grand, powerful and beautiful than we have ever imagined. And yes, that means you! How magnificent you are! You hold the power to change the world.

It Only Takes One More Drop

A very small number of people can have a huge effect on the mental and emotional climate of the world. Ever heard of the butterfly effect? A butterfly flapping its wings on one side of the world can cause a tornado at the other side. This has been proven mathematically.

Have you heard of the 'Hundredth Monkey' experiment? It took place in 1952, when a group of scientists was studying the behaviour of monkeys on the island of Koshima, off the coast of Japan. The monkeys were fed by dropping sweet potatoes on the sand, but the sand made the potatoes difficult to eat and eroded the monkeys' teeth. Soon, one of the monkeys learned to wash the potatoes in the ocean and then taught some of the others to do the same. As you would expect, the practice of washing the potatoes gradually spread throughout the group. But at one point, all of a sudden, every monkey in the group started washing its food.

At the same time, an unrelated group of scientists studying monkeys on the mainland also noticed an odd change in behaviour. All of a sudden, every one of the monkeys they were studying began to wash their food.

The two groups were not in contact, so there was no physical way for the second band of monkeys to have learned the practice from the first group. The idea of washing food had been transmitted through the monkeys' group consciousness.

This type of phenomenon has been well documented. In another experiment, two sets of laboratory rats were bred through several generations by biologist W. E. Agar, in Melbourne, Australia, and were kept apart so that there was never any contact between them. One set was trained to find their way through a maze and the other set was not. The rats that were trained to run through the maze took 25 attempts, on average, to get through it before they memorized the route. Each successive generation learned the way slightly faster than the preceding ones, and this was attributed, at the time, to learned behaviour being genetically inherited through the DNA.

By the fiftieth generation the rats were getting through the maze much faster. At this point the group of rats that had not been trained, also now in the fiftieth generation, was tested on the maze. One would expect these rats to take about 25 attempts, as had the first generation of the other group. However, it was discovered that they made it through as fast as the rats that had 'genetically inherited' the ability to run through the maze. Yet the two groups had never met. There was no genetic opportunity for the second group to inherit the knowledge. Once again, it had been transmitted through the group consciousness, so that when the untrained rats were tested on the maze, the knowledge was 'in the air' as part of the mental and emotional climate in the area. They just downloaded it.

Similarly, you may have noticed that when computers were first invented people found it difficult to understand them. Nowadays they are far more complex, yet people master them very quickly, particularly children. The knowledge has been passed along through the collective consciousness, so each successive generation of people is more confident with computers and has an innate basic awareness of them that is awakened when they begin to use them. Each user of a computer adds to the knowledge that is in the collective consciousness.

You might think of it as each user adding a layer of watercolour to a canvas. In time the colour becomes very deep and highly visible, even at a distance. In the same way, the understanding of computers forms a print in the collective consciousness that becomes more 'visible' with each successive generation.

Of course, in this case there are no isolated groups under study, like Agar's rats, so the learned behaviour is also genetically transmitted. Both ways of transmission occur.

Another thing that probably occurs is that information in the collective consciousness causes genes to switch on and off, perhaps altering the growth of the brain in such a way that makes it easier to understand technology. These genes may even have switched on and off in the womb.

Information travels fast through the collective unconscious and the collective mental and emotional climate. It is instantly available everywhere. But it usually takes a little while to be downloaded because of people's personal mental and emotional 'noise' – their thoughts and emotions, attitudes and beliefs – just as it takes someone longer to understand about something if they have a lot on their mind.

Usually information is gradually downloaded into more and more people until a 'critical' or 'tipping' point is reached. Then the information appears to download into everyone else simultaneously.

This is how critical points work. Levels increase gradually until a specific point is reached, then change is extremely rapid. Think of more and more weight being added to a set of scales. When the weight reaches the tipping point, the scales tip over to the other side.

This process is well known in meteorology, as sudden weather changes occur due to the reaching of a critical point of air pressure, storm density, wind speed or temperature. In the Hollywood movie *The Day After Tomorrow*, a tipping point is reached in polar icecap melting. After that there is no turning back. In just over a week the entire planet is in an ice age.

Certain types of biological experiments also show the tipping-point process. Bacterium A is slowly transforming into B, then all of a sudden, at a certain point, it flicks over to completion. In some cases, the critical amount can be very small and in other cases it can be large. Many vital protein and enzyme transformations in the body happen in this way.

Analytical chemists also see this process at work. They use 'indicators' which detect when an acid–alkali titration is complete. This is a standard experiment that is carried out from high schools to university research labs to analytical laboratories in the healthcare industry. Lots of drops of substance A can be added to substance B and the mixture remains colourless, then suddenly, with the addition of only one or two more drops of A, the entire mixture turns pink – an instant change.

So it is with the mixture of our mental and emotional climates. If we consistently add drops of peace and love, kindness and sharing, tolerance and understanding, through our attitudes and our behaviour towards each other, then once we reach a critical point, the world will change very quickly.

Just prior to the tipping point it only takes one more drop for the colour to change. Without that drop it never changes. So every drop is important. And you wondered how important you were!

Inspiring Peace

You don't need to do big things to change the world – you only need to change yourself. A determined positive attitude creates good health and positive life experiences, and when many of us focus our thoughts in this way it inspires positive world events.

The same, of course, happens when we dwell on what is not desirable. Focusing on your distaste for war and the decisions surrounding it, for example, will not bring lasting peace. Although you intend peace, you also feed the conflict. A love of peace and a demonstration of peace in your own life are a more efficient formula for lasting peace. The peace you create within yourself then inspires you to speak and behave differently, which has a knock-on effect on everyone you come into contact with, and it vibrates through the web, inspiring peace in other people and other places.

Tolerance and willingness to try to understand the actions of another also make more of a lasting contribution towards peace than a desire for peace that is fuelled by a hatred of war and all that it represents. St Francis of Assisi once said, 'Seek first to understand, then to be understood.' This is the key to peace in your personal life and in the world. Seek first to understand people before making a judgement, especially as you probably don't know all of the facts. Many of us have unknowingly perpetrated conflicts through making assumptions.

If you find yourself consistently reacting angrily to something or someone, try to stop for a minute and ask yourself what contribution such behaviour makes to the quality of your life or to the world. Then find a way of healing your thoughts, attitudes and beliefs.

The next time you find yourself speaking negatively about someone behind their back, stop and ask yourself what you will be doing to them, and what contribution your words are making to your life and to the world. You know what you do to your body with consistent negative thinking, so what do you suppose we do to the world every day when millions of us focus on the negative and go through our days in mental and emotional conflict with one another?

We are all intimately connected to every atom of the universe. We are all important and our thoughts, feelings and words are extremely powerful. Who we choose to be from this moment onwards will affect the world.

So who do you choose to be?

12
DNA II

We learned earlier that our Higher Selves create the subatomic particles that form our atoms, which then go on to form our proteins, enzymes and DNA, as well as the entire physical structure of our bodies. DNA is the genetic blueprint that determines what we look like, but the Higher Self provides the mental blueprint that precedes it and determines the physical structure of the DNA.

Many people believe that the mind is the product of chemical interactions in the brain. Indeed, scientific studies have shown that alterations to the brain cause perception and behavioural changes. But this is only half of the story. The mind *is* influenced by chemical interactions in the brain, but it originates *beyond* biology. I believe that the spirit flows *through* the body. Its flow is affected by the state of the body, giving us the impression that it is a product of biology.

I also believe that our genetic blueprint acts as a filter that allows a certain intensity of spirit (Higher Self) to influence the body and mind. The Higher Self chooses the genetic filter so that a life may be experienced within a certain context. We still have free will, of course.

Life, then, is a bit like a painting. The Higher Self chooses the canvas and the colours, but we create the picture. The mental blueprint of the Higher Self condenses into the chosen 'colours' of the DNA. Its thought waves (vibrations) condense into particles that form patterns that organize into matter that become the genes of the DNA.

Prior to the vibrations there is stillness, just like still water when there is no wind. In this state, nothing exists except perfect stillness. But then an idea arises and, just as a pebble dropped into water produces waves, it forms vibrations in the 'field' which then condense to form the particles that eventually produce the image of the idea. These vibrations are the mental blueprint that determines what you will look like, and the condensed particles organize themselves accordingly so that the appropriate genes are present in your DNA when you are no more than a single cell in the womb. These genes are predisposed to switch on and off so that you can grow into the image held by your Higher Self.

The new science of string theory, which many scientists believe could be the 'theory of everything', or at least point towards it, also talks of vibrations. These are likened to the vibrations of a violin string and are considered to be the real nature of subatomic particles. In other words, subatomic particles are not solid – they are really vibrations. Therefore, since subatomic particles make up everything, we can say that vibrations make up everything.

I believe that vibrating strings ultimately represent the intentions of God (or the equivalent in other spiritual and religious traditions) and that some also represent the intentions of our Higher Selves.

The genes that we are born with are principally the result of the choice of our Higher Selves. But they are also inherited from our parents. There is no contradiction here. Similarities probably exist in families because the Higher Selves have chosen to be similar. It may be that our human families are families of Higher Selves who think alike and so form similar vibrations. What we see as similar genes, in accordance with the laws of genetics and inheritance, may be no more than the end product of a creative series of events that originated with similar ideas. I believe that each Higher Self chooses particular genes within the framework of what is possible within such laws.

We are born, therefore, with certain genes that are predisposed to switch on at certain times throughout our lives to make our bodies look as they do and work as they do and to lead us into the types of experiences desired by our Higher Selves. You could say that the instructions for our unique mental, physical and spiritual growth – the mental blueprints – are imprinted onto our DNA.

Anyone can become aware of some of these mental blueprints, or imprints, as you might call them, particularly the ones relating to our purpose in life. Do you ever feel that you have a purpose that you are just not carrying out? Such feelings are the blueprints of the Higher Self.

I believe that carrying out – or 'living' – your purpose allows the maximum flow of the Higher Self through the body, and that is why people who are doing so tend to feel joyful most of the time.

Your purpose doesn't need to be something big. As people begin to embrace spiritual concepts they quite often feel that their purpose is to change the world single-handed, but this is usually just their newfound awareness of the awesome power of consciousness available to them. From my own experience there is often an increased flow of energy through the body at this time and there is undoubtedly a new program of genes switching on and off.

Your purpose may be subtle or it may have an obviously huge impact on the world. Many people's purpose is to bring children into the world. Others choose to act, to write books, to teach, to sing, to dance, to cook, to clean, to heal, to be peaceful, to cause chaos, to lead or to follow.

Parents will usually notice that their children have certain abilities from an early age. They might be highly intelligent, or great at sports, or really creative, or good mimics, or they might act like little doctors or nurses or teachers. Some might be fascinated by cars, or why things work the way they do. This is no accident. It is their purpose beginning to express itself.

In fact we usually have more than one purpose. As we fulfil one, the next takes precedence.

Why not ask your Higher Self what your purpose is? It may come to you in a flash of inspiration or you may find events just nudge you into doing whatever it is you are meant to do.

Conscious Evolution

Vibrations are consistent throughout the physical world. The Earth rotates about the sun, forming the cycle (vibration) of one year, the moon rotates about the Earth, forming the cycle of one month, and the Earth rotates on its axis, forming the cycle of one day.

Our bodies also work in cycles. In the science of genetics it is well known that many genes switch on and off in waves according to clock rhythms and cycles, for example the genes that are involved in sleep. Our growth is also determined by cycles. The brain, for instance, undergoes cyclic spurts of growth at birth and approximately at ages 1, 4, 7, 11, 15 and 21, each spurt involving waves of gene expression. The growth of the central nervous system has also been shown to take place through periodic waves of gene expression. Puberty and menopause are the results of longer-term cycles.

I believe that our internal body cycles are also ultimately a product of the Higher Self's thought vibrations. These vibrations will ultimately be the reason why certain genes are predisposed to switch on and off at specific times.

The very idea of the human race was once a vibration in the stillness of the field. You could call it the 'vibration of the human race'. This vibration ensures consistency in human DNA. It explains why most of us have two arms, two legs, two eyes, a mouth etc.

What we call serious genetic mutations, and the associated deformities, are not mistakes. In fact they must be the results of decisions by Higher Selves. A person who is physically or mentally different, whether due to a genetic difference or otherwise, should therefore never be considered less than anyone else. I believe that it takes a brave and enlightened soul to choose genetic characteristics that cause it to be labelled 'different' in unenlightened times.

What is normal is not what is right. It is just what most Higher Selves have chosen – no more, no less.

The human race has evolved over millions of years, so the vibration of the human race has been constantly changing in small ways. Vibrations can become either faster or slower – in other words, higher or lower. According to some spiritual traditions our collective vibration is, in fact, speeding up, which we see as tolerance, kindness and compassion flooding through the world in greater amounts than ever before.

As we embrace these values, the collective mental and emotional climate changes, sending intentions to the point where vibrations condense into particles. They then resonate with the vibration of the human race in much the same way that a tuning fork will cause a guitar string to vibrate to its tone. And as they resonate with it they begin to raise it to a higher vibration, just as a large pendulum entrains smaller ones to its rhythm. Since we can influence the collective mental and emotional climate in many ways, this gives us a degree of influence upon our own evolution.

As we collectively make choices based upon spiritual principles like tolerance, kindness and compassion, we produce higher vibrations that in turn entrain the collective vibration to a higher frequency. Each time, the string of humanity plays a higher note.

It goes the other way too. As the collective vibration increases in frequency it inspires *us*, influencing the choices we make, so that even more tolerance, kindness and compassion flow through the world. Look at the world – it is really obvious.

And each time the vibration shifts, it is not only our thoughts and emotions that are affected. Biology must shift too.

Of course I am not talking of obvious physical changes, although these might await us in the very distant future. I am referring to minor alterations in which genes are on and off (and some minor mutations – SNPs – that occur regularly and naturally), leading to relatively minor biological changes.

These will mirror the way in which we view each other and our place in the world.

It must be happening in people alive at present, and this may explain some of the changes we are seeing. Some people, for instance, are finding that their bodies no longer tolerate old eating habits and are developing unexplained allergies to foods that are unhealthy. Others find themselves experiencing greater psychological stress as the new vibration brings to the surface mental and emotional issues that need resolving. Some people are experiencing stress-related illnesses as they resist the inner urge to embrace their life's purpose. Others are simply feeling better and better every day.

All the *apparently* negative psychological and physical experiences are simply psychological and biological adjustments to the higher vibration and may be viewed as 'healing in progress'.

What is also really interesting is that the higher vibration will also influence people's DNA in the future because that DNA will condense from the vibration of the human race. So, if we choose more tolerance, kindness, compassion and peace, our children will be born with a greater predisposition towards love, peace and spiritual growth. And because this will affect the activation of some genes, the predisposition will even be written into the physical structure of the brain and will therefore also be manifest in the body. In this way, our choices today affect the future health and state of the world.

Each of us therefore has a great responsibility, not only to ourselves but also to our children. We can give them the chance to live in a world free of poverty, war and injustice, a world filled with sharing, co-operation, tolerance, compassion, achievement, education, kindness and peace.

I have heard stories – and I believe some of them because it makes sense in the context of what I have written here – that a number of children are being born with a higher level of immunity to some of our most serious diseases. This may be explained in purely genetic terms, but consciousness precedes biology. If the vibration level of humanity had evolved, say, 20 points in the last 20 years, then children being born now would have slightly different DNA, in terms of which genes are on and off, from children born 20 years ago. I am quite sure that scientists could find ways to verify this.

As we are collectively gaining a wiser spiritual understanding, we are slowly transcending old mental and emotional habits. It follows, therefore, that we are probably also developing physical resistance to some of the diseases that collectively mirrored these old habits. Many of us may have developed an immunity that we may never realize we have. Researchers looking for chemical or biological cures for some diseases may need to look no further than healthy people.

Group Illnesses

Epidemics can spread quickly around the world. But it can be the mind more than anything that helps in their spread. Many of us secretly believe that we will catch whatever disease is going. This is aided by advertisements that proclaim: 'One in three people will catch ... in their lifetime.'

Of course, advertisements of this nature are not intended to cause disease. It is the exact opposite – drugs manufacturers and research and development scientists are trying to help sick people. Their advertisements are not created with any conscious awareness of the 'disease suggestions' that they give to people. They simply use current statistics, but statistics can be misleading if they are not fully understood. They can create a local or global emotional climate that inspires people to believe that they will contract a certain disease. Then their body's biochemistry mirrors their belief, switching on viruses and bacteria already present in the body, or generating 'ghost' symptoms, or even causing them to unconsciously 'call out' to airborne pathogens, so the statistics have a chance of becoming self-fulfilling.

Most of us have traces of most viruses and bacteria, even the deadliest ones, in our bodies. Yet they lie dormant, doing no harm. In fact they probably play a cameo role in keeping health and balance in the body. Believing a disease suggestion might, however, switch them on, turning a usually harmless virus into a deadly one. In some cases, it might not be so much the virus that is the disease as the thoughts, emotions and beliefs that activate it.

On a global scale, the spread of an epidemic could be intensified by the mental and emotional patterns of an entire nation or culture. This might be one of the reasons why families and groups of people sharing similar attitudes and beliefs often develop the same illnesses.

There are of course many direct causes for diseases that are unrelated to conscious thoughts and feelings, for example diet, toxins, poisons, genetic inheritance, transmitted viruses and bacteria and even electromagnetic fields, to name just a few. Consciousness does not always play a large role, just as there is not always a large placebo effect in the treatment of some illnesses. But, however large or small, it cannot be ignored.

Another aspect of the role of consciousness is that collective thoughts can affect people all over the world, So our collective mental and emotional patterns might unconsciously project an illness, or the symptoms of an illness, world-wide.

For instance, atmospheric pollution and the destruction of oxygen-producing rainforests are currently damaging the 'lungs' of the planet. On an unconscious level we are all aware of this, because the knowledge vibrates the web. In an individual, consistent thoughts of damaged lungs might bring about such a condition, or the symptoms of the condition, in that person. So, collectively, we might expect to see an increase in the number of respiratory diseases (e.g. asthma or TB) all over the world. Most of the people with these diseases would not have attracted the illness through any conscious thought of their own, but the collective mental and emotional climate would have played a part.

In the same way, there might be a link between the reduction of the planet's biodiversity due to the man-made extinction of species, which damages the 'immune system' of the planet, and an increase in the number of people developing suppressed immune systems, allergies and related diseases. Again, the conscious and unconscious awareness of these events can be projected outwards and show up in people anywhere in the world, since we are all connected. And again, those affected did not attract the disease through any fault of their own, though their Higher Self undoubtedly had a reason for them to have developed it.

Just as we can attract diseases, however, we should also be able to deactivate them. Perhaps we can collectively generate a 'positive placebo effect' based on the belief that we are healthy! Maybe the media could help. With faith, we would develop a degree of mental and therefore physical immunity to new or existing diseases.

As mentioned earlier, as a consequence of our evolution in consciousness some people may already be psychologically and therefore physically immune to some diseases, and even if they contract them through the air they will immediately neutralize them. Such individuals are likely to exist, it is just that we are not generally aware of them and neither are they aware of their own immunities.

There is a habitual tendency in many of us only to notice something when it goes wrong and to give little attention to things that are going right. We often focus more on disease than health. But we get what we concentrate on, so we would do better to focus more on health and the reasons why people are healthy.

Our health, and our world, is in our hands. So let us appreciate each other and be kind to each other, and collectively we can make our world into an even more beautiful place.

13
Personal Responsibility

Each of us plays an important role in the world, regardless of our status, how much money we have, where we live, what we do for a living, whether we are married or single, whether we have children or whether we are children.

Every one of our thoughts, emotions, ideas and dreams contributes to the landscape of humanity. Together we make the world the way it is. In the grand scheme of things there is no one more important or less important than you, only people with different roles. Everyone's presence on the planet adds to the collective consciousness. Everyone is important.

It is not unusual to look at someone and think, 'How magnificent you are.' But there is someone, somewhere, looking in your direction thinking that about you.

If we want the world to be different, it is up to us to take responsibility for it. Each of our intentions, positive or negative, contributes to the whole and changes it in some way, just as creating a website changes the information content of the internet.

Every thought and emotion, value and belief, idea and dream is valid, even seemingly negative ones. It is not always harmful to have negative thoughts or painful emotions, even though we are well aware of their effects. It is often the case that people experience pain in order to jump up into a positive state. The challenging experience of pain can help us to grow.

It is important, also, not to judge a person acting from a negative space. To do so is to show a lack of compassion for another's pain and also to condemn yourself! Everyone has a place in the world and together we make it exactly the way it is.

If we want to make lasting changes in the world, consistency is the key. What we consistently project has a more lasting effect. So, if you want to see the world you dream of, first examine the contents of your own mind and take note of what you are projecting on a consistent basis. Second, work on resolving your own personal suffering. And finally, bring your thoughts, attitudes and actions into alignment with what you wish to see in the world.

Each of us, individually, is much more important and powerful than we believe. It is because most of us don't realize this that we keep on thinking and behaving in the same way. If, however, we can learn to consistently see the world through wiser eyes, seeing the beauty of nature and the inner beauty of all people, then we will create more beauty. This can be the legacy that we leave for our children.

Many of us condemn events that are undesirable, berating 'people' for not doing anything to change things while never realizing that we have a constant hand in their creation. Our attitude provides the food that nourishes the people doing the very things we disapprove of. We would do better to simply notice what is undesirable and then say that we love whatever the opposite might be. For example, seeing war as undesirable, you might want to say 'I love peace' and then be peaceful in your interactions with people. Also, try to focus on examples of peace in your personal life and in the world, because what you focus on you get more of.

It would also be good to search for the place within yourself that houses forgiveness, and practise forgiving people for any wrongs you believe they have done to you or to the world.

If you have difficulty in doing any of these things then seek a suitable resource, book, counsellor, therapist or teacher who can guide you in changing your inner beliefs, because it is our inner beliefs that cause us to think and act in particular ways. One such book I would recommend is *Loving What Is* by Byron Katie.

Being mindful like this is taking personal responsibility for your own life and for the part you play in the world. This is important, because you are an inspiration to people all over the world, even if you don't realize it. Who you choose to be today will impact on the people you come into contact with and, through the web, the people you do not. It is who you choose to be now that matters.

So who do you choose to be?

14
Three Simple Rules

There are three simple rules you can live by that can make you happy, inspire happiness in those around you and change the world. These are: love for self, love for others and love for nature.

Rule 1: Love for Self

Have you ever said to someone 'I love you just the way you are'? If you have, I bet you meant it, because we have a great capacity to see the best in each other. Love for self is saying 'I love myself just the way I am.' Or even, if you find this difficult, 'I am willing to try to find a way to move in this direction.'

Quite often, in trying to change ourselves, we beat ourselves up and dislike ourselves. And this sometimes makes us depressed. So love for self would also mean that it's OK to feel how you feel right now. Some people who have gone through depression have found that this is a good place to start.

Love for self also means to try to stop criticizing yourself. Try to stop beating yourself up for what you should or shouldn't have done. And try to stop blaming yourself for things that have happened in the past. A child learns from its mistakes but shouldn't be condemned for making them. It was a part of the process of learning, of evolution. In the grander scheme of things, we are all children and will inevitably make mistakes. It's part of the process.

I once heard Dr Wayne Dyer tell a story of how trappers used to catch monkeys in the jungle. They would set down a large heavy jar containing sweet nuts in an area where monkeys lived. The jar had a narrow neck just wide enough for a monkey's arm so that it could reach in to take the nuts. When a monkey came along it would reach into the jar and grab the nuts. But its tightening grip would make its hand too wide to get out of the jar. It would try and try, but it couldn't get its hand out of the jar unless it let go of the nuts. But it wouldn't let go of the nuts, even though it was stuck. And the jar was so heavy that it couldn't drag it to a different place. The trappers would return the next day and find the monkey still with its hand in the jar. It had been there all night, never having let go of the nuts and therefore being unable to move.

This is what we tend to do in our personal lives. We hold on to things that happened in the past, playing them over and over in our minds, blaming ourselves or others and refusing to let go. But this makes us heavy and unable to move forward in our lives. We trap ourselves.

Forgiveness is key. This doesn't mean you have to condone the actions of another person, only to forgive them. Doing this frees you to move on.

My friend Bruce MacKay once said to me while we were in the mountains of Peru, 'Where are you?' Bemused and trying to be funny, I said something along the lines of 'I am on a path in the mountains of Peru.' To this he replied, 'No. You are here.'

He then said, 'What time is it?' As I looked at my watch, he said, 'It is now. You are here, and the time is now.'

We tend to waste a lot of time in life by mulling over past events or by worrying about the future, but there is only one time: *now*. In ten minutes' time it will be a new now, but it will still be now. The present moment is where you are. And in this moment, you are deeply loved. You don't need to wait until some future time to be loved or until you have committed 100 selfless acts. If love is the guiding hand of all things, then you are loved now, you have always been loved and you will always be loved.

If I pointed to someone and said that they were created out of nothingness with a breath of pure love, what would you think? How would you regard them? I bet you would see them as a truly divine being, a wonderful spiritual being with the destiny to bring more love into the world. Well, I am pointing at you. You are that person! You were created with loving breath. This love is in every cell of your body.

I once heard a story about a woman who was feeling depressed, unloved and unimportant. One day, a friend came to her house and learned how she felt. He felt compassion for her. His attention was then drawn to the pictures on her mantelpiece, so he asked about them. The woman smiled as she explained that they were her children and grandchildren. She lit up as she described how proud she was of them and listed their achievements. Her friend then looked at her and said, 'God has a picture of you on his mantelpiece.'

It doesn't ultimately matter what you own, what you have accomplished or what you do in life. You are important just because you exist.

There's a little trick that can help you to develop love for yourself. It is called 'being kind to yourself', and it's fun.

Treat yourself to what you really want. Spoil yourself. Take a long bath with some candles and oils burning around you. Have a massage or have a healing treatment. Get your hair done or get a new image. If you don't have the resources or ability to do these things then try to find something really special that is possible for you. Maybe there's something you love to do but haven't done for a while.

As you do whatever it is you want , do so with the thought, 'I am a great and wonderful divine being. I am deeply loved, I love myself and I deserve this.'

Rule 2: Love for Others

We have an amazing capacity to see the best in each other. So, as often as you can, try to see the best in the person right in front of you. See the best in family members, friends, work colleagues, people you come into contact with throughout the day, people at meetings, clients, children, even people you regard as enemies and people who have hurt you in the past.

When you make an effort to see the best in someone, you help to bring it out in them. I used to be an athletics coach and I could only bring out the best in the athletes when I made an effort to recognize their uniqueness. When I saw it I could point it out to them. So it became more obvious and they were able to develop it. And they felt great because I had complimented them. It works the same way with qualities of character.

If someone told you that you were a generous person, for instance, after some thought, and maybe some mental replaying of past times, you would probably think to yourself, 'Hey, I *am* a generous person,' and with that thought foremost in your mind you would probably go through your day being even more generous than normal and touching many lives along the way. Pointing out great qualities in people can change the world.

To start with, you could notice, say, that someone occasionally showed kindness. Then you could try to let that be how you defined them in the future. You might say 'Oh, there goes that kind person' instead of 'There goes so and so. Have you heard the gossip?' My friend Stuart Wilkie used to say, 'If you have nothing nice to say then don't say anything at all.' 'It's nice to be nice,' as they say.

How you label a person is not who they are, of course. It is just your label, based upon your limited connection with them. You might not know them very well. But you can always make time to see something positive in someone that might help them to feel better about themselves. You might notice that they are a great parent, or a good communicator, or that they have a nice smile, or nice hair, or are wearing nice clothes today. Be creative.

Sometimes it might be difficult to see something positive in a person's behaviour, because circumstances have influenced some people so much that the positive part of them is buried. You can look for it. Help them to find it.

Sometimes behaviour can cloud the truth. But no matter how many clouds are there, the human spirit never ceases to shine from behind them. The actress Elizabeth Caproni, my partner, reminded me once that an aeroplane might take off on a cloudy day, but as it rises above the clouds it reaches a place where the sun always shines. She pointed out that everyone is beautiful on the inside. This natural love always shines from within. It's just that we don't always notice it. It is up to you to rise above the clouds that might be facing you and see it.

The actor David Hayman, a dear friend of mine, once said to me, while describing someone who brought lots of conflict into the room with him, 'He is an angel of God – cleverly disguised as an asshole.'

So, which part of a person are you willing to see? The part you focus on is the part you will then see most and will tease out of them.

If a person has hurt you in the past, try to forgive them, let it go and see their 'light from within'. As Mark Twain wrote, 'Forgiveness is the fragrance that the violet sheds on the heel that has crushed it.' Why not choose to be a violet today?

In 2004 I read in a national newspaper that a brother and sister had written to a judge who was about to pass sentence on the driver of a truck who had killed their parents in an accident. It was a plea to him not to imprison the driver. The letter brought tears to the judge's eyes as he read it aloud in court, emphasizing the extraordinary capacity for forgiveness that the brother and sister had shown.

If all of us followed their example the world would transform overnight. Overnight! We would surpass the 'forgiveness tipping point'. So, do you choose to forgive or do you choose to sue?

Forgiveness is a beautiful thing – as is kindness. Genuine kindness, in particular, carries extraordinary power. This is where you have nothing to gain from being kind and only wish to help. It is different from acting in order to gain something else. The vibration of the web is different. With a genuine act, the vibration of the web is greater.

Of course, it is not wrong to be aware that you will gain something from a kind act, because there will always be a gain for you. You cannot avoid that. You get back what you give out in one form or another. So if you give out kindness, you will receive kindness in some way. In fact, you receive the moment you give. Don't you feel great when you help someone?

But the real point is to be kind not in order to get something back but from a genuine heartfelt wish to help. Then your act carries much more weight. As my mum always tells me, 'It's the thought that counts.'

In the Bible it is written:

'I may speak with the words of men and of angels, but if I have not love I am but a resounding gong or a clanging cymbal.'
I Corinthians 13

To do something from a space of love carries real power. So examine your motivation!

Anonymous acts of kindness can also have a huge impact. There was a time, a few years ago, when I was extremely short of money. One day I received an envelope in the post containing £20. There was no name or address, only a small piece of paper with the words: 'God bless.' Whoever sent it knew of my situation but had no need for me to know of their kindness. They only wanted to help.

That £20 was like a lottery win to me, and it meant more and stretched further because of the love that came with it. The spirit of the gift was far more important to me than its monetary value. So it is with your genuinely kind thoughts, words and actions. The spirit of your intentions carries the power.

Have you ever seen the film *Pay It Forward*? It features a young boy who is set a school project to come up with a plan to make a difference in the world. His plan is to commit a very special act of kindness for three people, an act that can make a real difference in their lives. When each person wishes to show their gratitude he says that he doesn't want them to repay the kindness to him but to find three people whose lives they can make a difference in and to help them instead. Those people in turn will do something kind for three others, who will help three others, who will help three others, and so on. In this way they 'pay it forward'. It is a truly inspirational film and I encourage you to watch it or to read the book by Catherine Ryan Hyde. It shows the power a person has to make a real difference in the world through one or two simple acts of kindness.

The power to change the world is in you. It's in your ability to choose and your courage to follow through on your choices. All you need to do is choose to forgive and be kind, and you might just inspire others to do the same. A wave of forgiveness or kindness can be magical!

Rule 3: Love for Nature

In Thom Hartmann's bestselling book *The Prophet's Way*, he describes watching his teacher, Gottfried Müller, outside on the road at 5.30 a.m. picking up dozens of small earthworms that had come to the surface during the previous night's rainfall. He was giving them a few words of comfort and reassurance and returning them to the grass so that they wouldn't be run over by cars.

Herr Müller showed that love for these tiny helpless creatures was as important as love for other people. He had been carrying out these anonymous acts of compassion for years.

Compassion is compassion is compassion, regardless of

whom, or what, it is directed towards. And everything is part of nature. So extend the kindness and compassion you show for yourself and each other to animals and plants. Try to see the life and the beauty in nature all around you and you will help to bring it out into flower, so to speak.

How you choose to interact with nature, consistently, from this moment on, will impact your life and the world. Love is love is love regardless of whom, or what, you love. And every act colours the collective unconscious, vibrates the web and influences the world.

The question is, what type of world do you choose?

In Closing

Your thoughts are far more powerful than you have ever imagined them to be. They are the starting point of all change, and so the source of all change is within you. You have the power to change conditions inside your body and you have the power to change those outside it.

At times you may find that you are not able to change circumstances, but you nevertheless have a unique opportunity – to change yourself. Sometimes that's the whole point! And as you change yourself, the effects of the 'new you' vibrate throughout the entire world, making it a better place.

You are more beautiful than you have ever believed yourself to be. You are a part of God (or the equivalent in other spiritual and religious traditions) that can never, ever, be separate from God. This infinite source of all things is in every cell in your body and is revealed in every moment of your life.

Your Higher Self is a fragment of God that is simply more aware of its heritage than you are. It has encoded a general theme for your life into your DNA, and through this and other experiences you have an infinite number of unique opportunities to experience your godliness.

This theme is your life's purpose. Try to discover it. Look within yourself for what brings you most joy – that is where you will find it. Then, as you allow yourself to experience the feelings of joy, fascination, wonder, awe, excitement and enthusiasm that the idea of living your inspiration brings, you will find that things around you will change so that your dream becomes your reality.

And it is not only your own life that will be affected. Every thought, feeling, word or act sends ripples throughout the world, making a difference in the lives of other people.

But the most important aspect of your thoughts, feelings, words and actions is where they come from. Helping someone through genuine compassion, for instance, is far more powerful than doing so out of a sense of guilt or a desire to be recognized for your kindness. In the same way, intentionally crushing an insect has a destructive effect. It is the thought behind the act, however insignificant, that is important. It's the thought that counts.

So look at yourself honestly. Honestly! Examine your thoughts, feelings, attitudes, beliefs and behaviour. Then make any changes that you believe are necessary until what you project to the world is consistent with what you wish to see in the world.

The world will change as we change. It can't do anything else because it is part of us. Your degree of honesty with yourself will determine the speed of the changes and how profound they are. Eventually, as we learn to see God in ourselves, in everyone else and in every*thing* else, the changes will be massive.

To begin with, try to live by the three simple rules: love for self, love for others and love for nature. Try to see the love – the kindness, compassion, honesty, forgiveness and gratitude – all around you, regardless of how well it is hidden. See that the world is already beautiful and, in so doing, choose more of the beauty than the pain. You don't need to hate the pain. You only need to choose something else.

Choose love, choose peace, choose kindness, choose honesty and extend your hand in forgiveness and trust. Let these new choices colour the actions of your life from this day onwards. Then you will see the beauty and magnificence that are already present around you and you will believe that everything is indeed perfect.

Such faith can move mountains!

References

Chapter 1: Body and Mind

For the effects of positive and negative emotions on the heart and immune system, see:

R. McCraty, M. Atkinson, W. A. Tiller, G. Rein and A. D. Watkins, 'The effects of emotions on short-term power spectrum analysis of heart rate variability', *Am. Journal of Cardiology*, 1995, 76, 1089–93

G. Rein, M. Atkinson and R. McCraty, 'The physiological and psychological effects of compassion and anger', *J. Advancement in Med.*, 1995, 8(2), 87–105

Janice K. Kiecolt-Glaser, Lynanne McGuire, Theodore F. Robles and Ronald Glaser, 'Emotions, morbidity, and mortality: New perspectives from psychoneuroimmunology', *Annual Rev. Psychol.*, 2002, 53, 83–107

For general information on mind-body medicine, see Deepak Chopra, MD, *Quantum Healing: Exploring the Frontiers of Mind/Body Medicine* (Bantam, 1989), and Larry Dossey, MD, *Healing Beyond the Body* (Shambhala, 2001)

For the effect on the brain of reappraisal of a negative situation, see K. L. Phan, D. A. Fitzgerald, P. J. Nathan, G. J. Moore, T. W. Uhde and M. E. Tancer, 'Neural substrates for voluntary suppression of negative effect: A functional magnetic resonance imaging study', *Biol. Psychiatry*, 2005, 57, 210–19

For the effects of laughter on health, see:

- For a general review of the physiological effects of laughter: W. F. Fry, 'The physiological effects of humour, mirth, and laughter', *Journal of the American Medical Association*, 1992, 267(13), 1857–8

- Laughter improves the immune system. Increases found in natural killer cell activity and levels of some immunoglobulins, with immunoglobulin increases lasting up to 12 hours after the laughter in some cases, in L. S. Berk, D. L. Felton, S. A. Tan, B. B. Bittman and J. Westengard, 'Modulation of neuroimmune parameters during the eustress of mirthful laughter', *Alternative Therapies*, 2001, 7(2), 62–76

- For the effects of laughter on some hormone levels: L. S. Berk, S. A. Tan, W. F. Fry, B. J. Napier, J. W. Lee, R. W. Hubbard, J. E. Lewis and W. C. Eby, 'Neuroendocrine and stress hormone changes during mirthful laughter', *The American Journal of the Medical Sciences*, 1989, 298(6), 390–96

- For the story of Norman Cousins and his laughter-aided recovery from a serious illness: Norman Cousins, 'Anatomy of an illness', *New England J. Medicine*, 1976, 295, 1458–63. Norman discovered that 10 minutes of genuine belly laughter had an anaesthetic effect and allowed him about two hours of pain-free sleep.

For the physiological effects of meditation, see Paramahansa Yogananda, *Autobiography of a Yogi*, (Self-Realization Fellowship, 1946), and for the physiological effects and examples of meditation techniques, see Dharma Singh Khalsa, MD, *Meditation as Medicine* (Pocket Books, 2001)

The report of the effects of TM meditation on children with ADHD featured in the media in March 2006. It was conducted by Dr William Stixrud, a clinical neurophysiologist, and Sarina Grosswald, an expert in cognitive learning.

Botox is a snake venom that is used in cosmetic procedures to temporarily paralyze some of the muscles of the forehead. Through this paralysis it removes the appearance of wrinkles on the forehead and around the eyes by completely relaxing the muscles.

For the story of the man who visualized a healthy liver, see Carolyn Miller, PhD, *Creating Miracles* (H. J. Kramer, Inc., 1995)

For creative visualization techniques, see Shakti Gawain, *Creative Visualization* (Whatever, 1978), as well as Ed Bernd and Ian Pollock, *Silva Method* (Silva Method Publishing, 2001)

For a summary of 18 individual scientific studies linking suppressed negative emotion and cancer, see: James Gross, 'Emotional expression in cancer onset and progression', *Soc. Sci. Med.*, 1989, 28(12), 1239–48

For an early published correlation between personality type and the progression of cancer: E. Blumberg, P. West and F. Ellis, 'A possible relationship between psychological factors and human cancer', *Psychosom. Res.*, 1954, 16, 27–86

To see the relationship between Type C personality and tumour thickness: L. Temoshok, B. W. Heller, R. W. Sagebiel, M. S. Blois, D. M. Sweet, R. J. Di Clemente and M. L. Gold, 'The relationship of psychosocial factors to prognostic indicators in cutaneous malignant melanoma', *J. Psychosom. Res.*, 1985, 29, 139–54

For the positive effects of the release of suppressed negative emotion on cancer, see:

- J. W. Pennebaker, J. K. Kiecolt-Glaser and R. Glaser, 'Disclosure of traumas and immune function: Health implications for psychotherapy', *J. Consult. Clin. Psychol.*, 1988, 56, 239–45

- D. Spiegel, J. Bloom, H. C. Kramer *et al*, 'Effect of psychological treatment on survival of patients with metastatic breast cancer', *Lancet*, 1989, 2, 888–91

- A. L. Stanton, S. Danoff-Burg, L. A. Sworowski, C. A. Collins, A. D. Branstetter, A. Rodriguez-Hanley, S. B. Kirk and J. L. Austenfield, 'Randomized, controlled trial of written emotional expression and benefit finding in breast cancer patients', *J. Clin. Oncology*, 2002, 20(20), 4160–68

For the positive effects on asthma and rheumatoid arthritis, see J. M. Smyth, A. A. Stone, A. Hurewitz and A. Kaell, 'Effects of writing about stressful experiences on symptom reduction in patients with asthma or rheumatoid arthritis', *J. Am. Med. Assoc.*, 1999, 14, 1304–27

For the relationship between coming 'out of the closet' and HIV and AIDS progression, see S. W. Cole, M. E. Kemeny, S. E. Taylor, B. R. Visscher and J. L. Fahey, 'Accelerated course of human immunodeficiency virus infection in gay men who conceal their homosexual identity', *Psychosom. Med.*, 1996, 58, 219–31

For the story of Brandon Bays and her recovery from a basketball-sized tumour, see Brandon Bays, *The Journey* (Thorsons, 1999)

Chapter 2: The Power of Faith

For general examples and a description of the placebo effect, see Herbert Benson, *Timeless Healing: The Power and Biology of Belief* (Simon & Schuster, 1996)

For the study of the placebo and Parkinson's disease: F. Benedetti, L. Colloca, E. Torre, M. Lanotte, A. Melcarne, M. Pesare, B, Bergamasco and L. Lopiano, 'Placebo-responsive Parkinson patients show decreased activity in single neurons of subthalmic nucleus', *Nature Neuroscience*, 2004, 7, 587–8

For the placebo effect and morning sickness: S. Wolff, 'Effects of suggestion and conditioning on the action of chemical agents in human subjects: The pharmacology of placebos', *Journal of Clinical Investigation*, 1950, 29, 100–109

For the placebo effect and asthma: C. Butler and A. Steptoe, 'Placebo responses: An experimental study of psychophysiological processes in asthmatic volunteers', *British Journal of Clinical Psychology*, 1986, 25, 173–83

For the effect of colour on the placebo effect: G. S. Kienle and H. Kiene, 'Placebo effects from packaging, formulation, colour, and size of the placebo' in 'Placebo effect and placebo concept: A critical methodological and conceptual analysis of reports on the magnitude of the placebo effect', *Alternative Therapies,* 1996, 2, 39–54, cited in L. Dossey, *Healing Beyond the Body* (Shambhala, 2001)

For history of psychoneuroimmunology, the discovery of the opiate receptor and how neuropeptides and their receptors work, see Candace B. Pert, PhD, *Molecules of Emotion* (Scribner, 1997)

For summary papers on psychoneuroimmunology and the role of neuropeptides, see:

- C. B. Pert, H. E. Dreher and M. R. Ruff, 'The psychosomatic network: Foundations of mind-body medicine', *Alternative Therapies*, 1998, 4(4), 30–41

- C. B. Pert, M. R. Ruff, R. J. Weber and M. Herkenham, 'Neuropeptides and their receptors: A psychosomatic network', *J. Immunol.*, 1985, 35(2), 820s–26s

For the role of neuropeptides as informational substances, see F. D. Schmitt, 'Molecular regulation of brain function: A new view', *Neuroscience*, 1984, 13, 991

For the role of neuropeptides with emotional centres in the brain and in the immune system, see:

- M. R. Ruff, V. Schiffman, V. Terranova and C. B. Pert, 'Neuropeptides are chemoattractants for human tumour cells and monocytes: A possible mechanism for metastasis', *Clin. Immunol. Immunopathol.*, 1985, 37, 387–96

- M. R. Ruff, S. M. Wahl, S. Mergenhagen and C. B. Pert, 'Opiate receptor-mediated chemotaxis of human monocytes', *Neuropeptides*, 1985, 5, 363

For bi-directional communication between emotions and immune system, see D. J. Carr and J. E. Blalock, 'Neuropeptide hormones and receptors common to the immune and neuroendocrine systems: Bi-directional pathway of intersystem communication' in R. Ader, D. L. Felten and N. Cohen, eds, *Psychoneuroimmunology II* (Academic Press, 1991)

For neuropeptide approaches to cancer and AIDS, see Candace B. Pert, PhD, *Molecules of Emotion* (Scribner, 1997)

For the role of opioids in the placebo effect, see:

- J. D. Levine, N. C. Gordon and H. L. Fields, 'The mechanism of placebo analgesia', *Lancet*, 1978, 654–7

- F. Benedetti, M. Amanzio and G. Maggi, 'Potentiation of placebo analgesia by proglumide', *Lancet*, 1995, 346, 1231

- G. ter Riet, A. J. M. de Craen, A. de Boer and A. G. H. Kessels, 'Is placebo analgesia mediated by endogenous opioids? A systematic review', *Pain*, 1998, 76, 273–5

- F. Benedetti, A. Pollo, L. Lopiano, M. Lanotte, S. Vighetti and I. Rainero, 'Conscious expectation and unconscious conditioning in analgesic, motor, and hormonal placebo/nocebo responses', *J. Neuroscience*, 2003, 23(10), 4315–23

- A. Pollo, S. Vighetti, I. Rainero and F. Benedetti, 'Placebo analgesia and the heart', *Pain*, 2003, 102, 125–33

For PET scans of the brain during placebo analgesia, see J. K. Zubieta *et al*, 'Placebo effects mediated by endogenous opioid activity on u-opioid receptors', *J. Neuroscience*, 2005, 25(34), 7754–62

See also P. Petrovic, E. Kalso, K. M. Petersson and M. Ingvar, 'Placebo and opioid analgesia: Imaging a shared neuronal network', *Science*, 2002, 295, 1737–40, for brain-imaging scans of opioid versus placebo analgesia.

For a thorough summary of the molecular mechanisms of the placebo effect in the brain, see F. Benedetti, H. S. Mayberg, T. D. Wager, C. S. Stohler and J.-K. Zubieta, 'Neurobiological mechanisms of the placebo effect', *J. Neuroscience*, 2005, 25(45), 10390–402

Chapter 3: DNA

For the discovery of the double-helix structure of DNA, see J. Watson and F. Crick, 'A structure for deoxyribose nucleic acid', *Nature*, 1953, 171, 737

For the role played by Rosalind Franklin in the discovery of the structure of DNA, see Brenda Maddox, 'The double helix and the "Wronged Heroine" ', *Nature*, 2003, 421, 407–408

For a great book all about DNA, its discovery, modern applications and genetic technologies, see James Watson, *DNA: The Secret of Life* (Arrow Books, London, 2004)

For the role of interleukin-2 in recovery from cancer, see:

S. Rosenberg and J. Barry, *The Transformed Cell: Unlocking the Mysteries of Cancer* (Putnam/Chapmans, New York, 1992)

J. Newman, 'I have seen cancers disappear', interview with Steven Rosenberg, *Discover*, 2001, 22, 44–51

For the effect of touch on memory and mental abilities and therefore growth of the brain, see:

- N. Jutapakdeegul, S. O. Casalotti, P. Govitrapong and N. Kotchabhakdi, 'Postnatal touch stimulation acutely alters corticosterone levels and glucocorticoid receptor gene expression in the neonatal rat', *Developmental Neuroscience*, 2003, 25, 26–33

- K. A. Fenoglio, K. L. Brunson, S. Avishai-Eliner, B. A. Stone, B. J. Kapadia and T. Z. Baram, 'Enduring handling-evoked enhancement of hippocampal memory function and GR expression involves activation of the CRF type-1 receptor', *Endocrinology*, 2005, 146(9), 4090–96

- K. A. Fenoglio, Y. Chen and T. Z. Baram, 'Neuroplasticity of the hypothalamic-pituitary-adrenal axis early in life requires recurrent recruitment of stress-regulating brain regions', *J. Neuroscience*, 2006, 26(9), 2434–42

For the study showing a reduction of up to 40 per cent of previous growth hormone levels through deprivation of maternal touch, see S. Wang, J. Bartolome and S. Schanberg, 'Neonatal deprivation of maternal touch may suppress ornithine decarboxylase via downregulation of the protooncogenes c-myc and max', *J. Neuroscience*, 1996, 16(2), 836–42; also summarized in E. L. Rossi, 'Psychosocial genomics: Gene expression, neurogenesis, and human experience in mind-body medicine', *Advances*, 2002, 18(2), 22–30

For a summary of research in psychosocial genomics, see Ernest L. Rossi, *The Psychobiology of Gene Expression: Neuroscience and Neurogenesis in Hypnosis and the Healing Arts* (Norton, 2002)

See also:

- Ernest Rossi, 'Stress-induced alternative gene splicing in mind-body medicine', *Advances*, 2004, 20(2), 12–19

- Ernest Rossi, 'Gene expression, neurogenesis, and healing: Psychosocial genomics of therapeutic hypnosis', *American Journal of Clinical Hypnosis*, 2003, 45(3), 197–216

For information about nature vs nurture, including examples of the relative roles of genes and the environment in human growth and development, see Matt Ridley, *Nature via Nurture: Genes, Experience and What Makes Us Human* (Fourth Estate, 2003), and Tim Spector, *Your Genes Unzipped: How your Genetic Inheritance Shapes your Life* (Robson Books, 2003). These books were also the source of the figures for the differences in genes between humans and other species.

For some of Eric Kandel's work, see Eric R. Kandel, MD, 'A new intellectual framework for psychiatry', *American Journal of Psychiatry*, 1998, 155(4), 457–69

For general information about the role of the emotional environment in the growth of the prefrontal lobes in infants and children, see Joseph Chilton Pearce, *The Biology of Transcendence* (Park Street Press, 2002)

For a description of psychosocial dwarfism or nonorganic failure-to-thrive, see L. Gardner, 'Deprivation dwarfism', *Scientific American*, 1972, 227(1), 76–82

For studies on the effect of emotional deprivation and lack of touch on growth hormone levels, see:

- G. Powell, N. Hopwood and E. Barratt, 'Growth hormone studies before and during catch-up growth in a child with emotional deprivation and short stature', *J. Clin. Endocrinol. Metab.*, 1973, 37(5), 674–9

- G. Powell, J. Brasel and J. Hansen, 'Emotional deprivation and growth retardation simulating idiopathic hypopituitarism: I. Clinical evaluation of the syndrome', *New England J. Medicine*, 1967, 276(23), 1271–8

For the reversal of early negative effects in childhood, see T. W. Bredya, R. A. Humpartzoomian, D. P. Cain and M. J. Meaney, 'Partial reversal of the effect of maternal care on cognitive function through environmental enrichment', *Neuroscience*, 2003, 118(2), 571–6

For information about ADHD, see Thom Hartmann, *Attention Deficit Disorder: A Different Perception* (Underwood Books, 1997)

Although 99.9 per cent of our genes are known to be the same, at least three million natural subtle variations exist in the individual genes. These are known as 'single nucleotide polymorphisms' (SNPs) and it is believed that they give rise to some of our individuality.

Chapter 4: The Power of Intention

For research on the infectiveness of emotion, see H. Friedman and R. Riggio, 'Effect of individual differences in nonverbal expressiveness on transmission of emotion', *Journal of Nonverbal Behaviour*, 1981, 6(2), 96–104

For a summary of Bernard Grad's research on healing, see:

- Bernard R. Grad, 'Some biological effects of laying-on of hands: A review of experiments with animals and plants', *Journal of the American Society for Psychical Research*, 1965, 59, 95–127

- Bernard R. Grad, 'The laying on of hands: Implications for psychotherapy, gentling and placebo effect', *Journal of the American Society for Psychical Research*, 1967, 61, 286–305

For the effects of healing touch on enzymes, see:

- J. Smith, 'The influence on enzyme growth by the "laying on of hands" ', *The Dimensions of Healing: A Symposium*, The Academy of Parapsychology and Medicine, Los Altos, CA, 1972

- Toni Bunnell, 'The effect of "healing with intent" on pepsin enzyme activity', *J. Sci. Explor.*, 1999, 13(2), 139–48

For the effects on E-coli, see C. B. Nash, 'Test of psychokinetic control of bacterial mutation', *J. Am. Soc. Psychical Res.*, 1984, 78(2), 145–52

For the study of using qigong to influence human-cultured brain cells, see G. Yount, J. Solfvin, D. Moore, M. Schlitz, M. Reading, K. Aldape and Y. Qian, 'In vitro test of external qigong', *BMC Complementary and Alternative Medicine*, 2004, 4(5)

For a description of Paramahansa Yogananda's discussions with Luther Burbank, see Paramahansa Yogananda, *Autobiography of a Yogi* (Self-Realization Fellowship, 1946)

For a general understanding of and scientific studies on acupuncture, see Richard Gerber, MD, *Vibrational Medicine for the 21st Century* (Eagle Books, 2000)

For a summary of qigong research, see K. M. Sancier, 'Medical applications of qigong', *Alternative Therapies*, 1996, 2(1), 40–46

General healing by touch and intention references can be found in Daniel J. Benor, *Healing Research, Volume I: Spiritual Healing: Scientific Validation of a Healing Revolution* (Vision Publications, 2001)

Chapter 5: Good Vibrations

For a summary of the research into the effects of healing touch and intention on water by William Tiller and others, see William A. Tiller, PhD, *Science and Human Transformation: Subtle Energies, Intentionality, and Consciousness* (Pavior, 1997)

For the effect of a healer's hands on the infrared spectrum of water, see S. A. Schwartz, R. J. De Mattei, E. G. Brame Jr and J. P. Spottiswoode, 'Infrared spectra alteration in water proximate to the palms of therapeutic practitioners', *Subtle Energies*, 1990, 1(1), 43–72

The information on Dr Glen Rein's research into the effects of human intention on DNA was gained in a personal discussion with him. Some of his work is summarized in William Tiller's book listed above.

For general information about homoeopathy, Bach flower remedies and vibrational medicine, see Richard Gerber, MD, *Vibrational Medicine for the 21st Century* (Eagle Books, 2000)

For information about the vibrational solutions of a rock called Aulterra, see work by Kim Dandurand. Kim discovered that a highly paramagnetic rock substance called Aulterra and its vibrational essence produced by succussion in water had healing properties. General analysis showed this to be correct and showed that the rock energized water and food substances that it came into contact with or was held close to. Kirlian photographs also showed a powerful energy field emanating from the rock and from the food supplements that it was held close to. I have personally tested Aulterra and found that holding it close to water and then using that water on cress seeds caused an increase in their rate of growth in a seven-day experiment. For general information about Aulterra and some of the scientific studies, see www.aulterra.com.

For information on paramagnetism and its effects on biology and plants, see Philip S. Callahan, PhD, *Paramagnetism* (Acres USA, 1995)

For Jacques Benveniste's scientific paper showing the highly dilute effects of the anti-IgE antibody, see E. Davenas, F. Beauvais, J. Amara, M. Oberbaum, B. Robinzon, A. Miadonna, A. Tedeschi, B. Poweranz, P. Fortner, P. Belon, J. Sainte-Laudy, B. Poitevin and J. Benveniste, 'Human basophil degranulation triggered by very dilute antiserum against IgE', *Nature*, 1988, 333, 816–18

For further scientific evidence of the power of homoeopathy, see David Reilly, 'Is evidence for homeopathy reproducible?', *Lancet*, 1994, 344, 1601–1606

For some digital biology (electromagnetic molecular signalling (EMS)) research by Professor Jacques Benveniste, see:

- J. Benveniste, B. Arnoux and L. Hadji, 'Highly dilute antigen increases coronary flow of isolated heart from immunized guinea-pigs', *FASEB Journal*, 1992, 6, A1610

- J. Benveniste, J. Aissa and D. Guillonet, 'Digital biology: Specificity of the digitised molecular signal', *FASEB Journal*, 1998, 12, A412 (2392)

- J. Benveniste, P. Jurgens and J. Aissa, 'Digital recording/transmission of the cholinergic signal', *FASEB Journal*, 1996, 10, A1479

- Y. Thomas, M. Schiff, M. H. Litime, L. Belkadi and J. Benveniste, 'Direct transmission to cells of a molecular signal (phorbol myristate acetate, PMA) via an electronic device', *FASEB Journal*, 1995, 9, A227

- J. Aissa, M. H. Litime, E. Attias and J. Benveniste, 'Molecular signalling at high dilution or by means of electronic circuitry', *Journal of Immunology*, 1993, 150, 146A (830)

- J. Benveniste, L. Kahhak and D. Guillonet, 'Specific remote detection of bacteria using an electromagnetic/digital procedure', *FASEB Journal*, 1999, 13, A852 (645.22)

For information on digital biology and a full list of Professor Benveniste's papers, see www.digibio.com

For sending a digitized signal along a telephone line, see J. Benveniste, P. Jurges, W. Hsuch and J. Aissa, 'Transatlantic transfer of digitised antigen by telephone link', *J. Allergy and Clinical Immunology*, 1997, 99(1) part 2, S:175 (705)

For a summary of some of Jacques Benveniste's digital biology work, see Lynn McTaggart, *The Field*, (HarperCollins, 2001)

For the effect of some pieces of music on the immune system, see R. McCraty, M. Atkinson, G. Rein and A. Watkins, 'Music enhances the effect of positive emotional states on salivary Immunoglobulin A', *Stress Medicine*, 1996, 12, 167–75. The music that was found to have the largest immune-boosting effect was called *Heart Zones*. It was created by the Institute of Heartmath to create a calm but energetic alertness and aid mental and emotional balance.

For the effects of drumming on the immune system, see B. B. Bittman, L. S. Berk, D. L. Felten, J. Westengard, C. Simonton, J. Pappas and M. Ninehouser, 'Composite effects of group drumming music therapy on modulation of neuroendocrine-immune parameters in normal subjects', *Alternative Therapies*, 2001, 7(1), 38–47

The source of information on the studies of music on the heart and on premature babies was the BBC news website. The articles are: 'Music training good for heart' and 'Live music calms premature babies'. To see the articles, I would suggest a Google search of title of the article along with 'BBC'.

For information about the Japa meditation, see Wayne Dyer, *Getting in the Gap* (Hay House, 2003)

For Fabien Maman's research on the effects of sound on cancer cells, see www.tama-do.com

For information about use of sound in healing see www.soundintentions.com

For work on levels of consciousness, see David R. Hawkins, *Power vs Force* (Veritas Publishing, 1995)

Effects of words on the growth of cress seeds

Below is a summary list of my own research into the effects of words on the height of cress sprouts over the course of seven days. Each word was written on a label and stuck onto a cup. Water was then added to the cup and immediately used to water six pots of 50 seeds. Each measurement below represents the average seed height of 50 sprouts. The mean figures are therefore an average for 300 seeds.

	Love (height of sprouts in mm)	**Happy** (height of sprouts in mm)	**Fear** (height of sprouts in mm)	**Sad** (height of sprouts in mm)	**Control** (height of sprouts in mm)
Mean	45.39	46.06	42.43	40.14	43.34

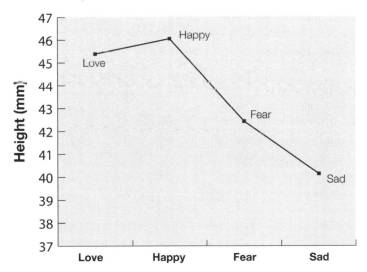

Height of Sprouts after 7 Days

For photographs of the effects of words, emotions and music on water crystals, see Masaru Emoto, *Messages from Water* (Hado, 1999) and *The Hidden Messages in Water* (Sumante Publishing Inc., 2001)

Chapter 6: Distant Healing and Prayer

Distant healing

For the effect of mental activation and calming of targets, see D. J. Radin, R. K. Taylor and W. G. Braud, 'Remote mental influence of human electrodermal activity: A preliminary replication', *Proceedings of the Parapsychological Association 36th Annual Conference*, 1993, 12–13

For a summary of the research on distant healing, see:

- Elisabeth Targ, 'Evaluating distant healing: A research review', *Alternative Therapies*, 1997, 3(6), 74–8

- Marilyn Schlitz and William Braud, 'Distant intentionality and healing: Assessing the evidence', *Alternative Therapies*, 1997, 3(6), 62–73

For a study of the effect of distant intention on hypertension, see R. N. Miller, 'Study on the effectiveness of remote mental healing', *Med. Hypoth.*, 1982, 8, 481–90

For a study of the distant effects on blood, see:

- William Braud, 'Distant mental influence of rate of hemolysis', *Research in Parapsychology*, 1989

- William Braud, 'Distant mental influence on rate of hemolysis of human red blood cells', *J. Am. Soc. Psychical Res.*, 1990, 84, 1–24

For the effect of distant healing on AIDS patients, see F. Sicher, E. Targ, D. Moore and H. S. Smith, 'A randomized double-blind study of the effect of distant healing in a population with advanced AIDS: Report of a small-scale study', *Western Medical Journal*, 1998, 169(6), 356–63

For distant intentional effects on fungus, see:

- J. Barry, 'General and comparative study of the psychokinetic effect on a fungus culture', *J. Parapsychology*, 1968, 32(4), 237–43

- W. Tedder and M. Monty, 'Exploration of long-distance PK: A conceptual replication of the influence on a biological system' in W. G. Roll *et al*, eds, *Research in Parapsychology*, 1980, 90–93

Information about increase in growth rate of rye grass at 500km can be found on an audiotape set by Richard Gerber, MD, *Exploring Vibrational Medicine*, (Sounds True, 1997)

For a study of distant influence on mental concentration, see W. Braud, D. Shafer, K. McNeill and V. Guerra, 'Attention focusing facilitated remote mental interaction', *Proceedings of the Parapsychological Association 36th Annual Conference*, 1993, 1–11

Prayer
For the effects of prayer on recovery from heart operations, see: Randolph C. Byrd, 'Positive therapeutic effects of intercessory prayer in a coronary care unit population', *Southern Medical Journal*, 1988, 81, 826–9

M. W. Krucoff, S. W. Crater, C. L. Green, A. C. Maas, J. E. Seskevich, J. D. Lane, K. A. Loeffler, K. Morris, T. M. Bashore, H. G. Koenig, 'Integrative noetic therapies as adjuncts to precutaneous intervention during unstable coronary syndromes: Monitoring and actualisation of noetic training (MANTRA) feasibility pilot', *American Heart Journal*, 2001, 142, 760–97

For experiments where people praying received as much benefit as the people they prayed for, see S. O'Laoire, 'An experimental study of the effects of distant intercessory prayer on self-esteem, anxiety, and depression', *Alternative Therapies*, 1997, 3(6), 38–53

For the effects of rosary prayer and yoga mantras on breathing and the heart, see L. Bernardi, P. Sleight, G. Bandinelli, S. Cencetti, L. Fattorini, J. Wdowczyc-Szulc and A. Lagi, 'Effect of rosary prayer and yoga mantras on autonomic cardiovascular rhythms: Comparative study', *British Medical Journal*, 2001, 323, 1446–9

For information on Tibetan praying techniques and prayer information from the Dead Sea Scrolls, see Gregg Braden, *The Isaiah Effect* (Harmony Books, 2000)

Chapter 7: The Nature of Reality

For information on quantum theory and the connectedness of all things, see:

- Jim Al-Khalili, *Quantum: A Guide for the Perplexed* (Weidenfeld & Nicholson, 2003)

- Will Arntz, Betsy Chasse and Mark Vicente, *What the Bleep Do We Know?* (DVD), Lord of the Wind Films, 2005

- J. S. Bell, 'On the Einstein-Podolsky-Rosen paradox', *Physics*, 1964, 1, 195–200

- A. Einstein, B. Podolsky and N. Rosen, 'Can quantum-mechanical description of physical reality be considered complete?', *Phys. Rev.*, 1935, 47, 777–80

- John Gribbin, *In Search of Scrödinger's Cat* (Black Swan, 1984)

- Brian D. Josephson and Fotini Pallikari-Viras, 'Biological utilization of quantum nonlocality', *Foundations of Physics*, 1991, 21(2), 197–207

- Euan J. Squires, 'Quantum theory and the relation between the conscious mind and the physical world', *Synthese*, 1993, 97, 109–23

- Gary Zukav, *The Dancing Wu Li Masters* (William Morrow, 1979)

There are obvious parallels between my description of condensing consciousness and the collapse of the wave function in theoretical quantum physics, also with Bell's Theorem and the theory of the primacy of consciousness – that consciousness is the basic building block of reality. I have made my own interpretations of the theories, which have led to the simplistic description that I present. Due to the complex nature of the subject, I chose a visibly simple method of describing reality that could be easily understood by most people.

Where I refer to there being 'nothing there' in the quantum field, I am referring to there being nothing physical – no physical matter. In actual fact the quantum field is seething with activity as particles pop in and out of existence.

For a metaphysical view, see Jane Roberts, *The Nature of Personal Reality (A Seth Book)*, (Prentice-Hall, 1974)

For information on the primacy of consciousness and how consciousness is the building block of reality, see Amit Goswami, PhD, *The Self-Aware Universe: How Consciousness Creates the Material World* (Tarcher/Penguin, 1995)

For information about chaordic businesses and chaordic management, see Dee Hock, *Birth of the Chaordic Age* (Berret-Koehler, 1999)

Chapter 8: Experiments in Connectedness

For a good summary of research using random-event generators and for work on ESP, see Dean I. Radin, *The Conscious Universe* (HarperCollins, 1997)

For a summary of the PEAR Group research at Princeton University, see B. J. Dunne and R. G. Jahn, 'Consciousness, information, and living systems', *Cellular and Molecular Biology*, 2005, 51, 703–14

For information about decreased crime rate in cities, see *Journal of Crime and Justice*, 1981, 4, 25–45, and for information about reduced terrorism and international conflict, see 'Time Series impact-assessment analysis of reduced international conflict and terrorism: Effects of large assemblies of participants in the transcendental meditation and TM-Sidhi programs', paper

References

presented at the American Political Science Association AGM, Atlanta, Georgia, August 1989, For details of similar scientific studies, see the website of the Maharishi University of Management, www.mum.edu

For information on the charity Spirit Aid, see www.spiritaid.org.uk. The original Spirit Aid event was titled 'World Energy Day' and was intended for October 2001. As more people joined the organizing team the name changed and the event was rescheduled for July 2002 in a football stadium. However, funding challenges led to its taking the form of a 9-day, 24-event festival of peace featuring scaled-down elements of the originally planned event. The festival also included a peace walk up a Scottish mountain (Ben Lomond), a conference, a concert, a peace procession through the city, talks, workshops, a picnic for peace and meditations, and the children of Glasgow made 50 metres of James Twyman's 'Children's Cloth of Many Colours' where they each wrote a peace message on a small piece of cloth that was then sewn onto the main cloth.

For information about James Twyman, see www.emissaryoflight.com

For information about Gregg Braden, see www.greggbraden.net

For information about Doreen Virtue, see www.angeltherapy.com

For a summary of ESP experiments between 1964 and 1993, see Julie Milton, 'Ordinary state ESP meta analysis' in *Proceedings of the Parapsychological Association 36th Annual Conference*, M. J. Schlitz, ed., 1993

For the effect of hypnosis on ESP ability, see R. G. Stanford and A. G. Stein, 'A meta-analysis of ESP studies contrasting hypnosis and a comparison condition', *Journal of Parapsychology*, 1994, 58(3), 235–70

For the effect on ESP of belief, and also the effect of hypnosis, see L. Casler, 'The improvement of clairvoyant scores by means of hypnotic suggestion', *Journal of Parapsychology*, 1962, 26, 77–87. The paper suggests that people block their ESP and clairvoyant abilities because of 1) fears of social ridicule, and 2) early learning that this is not possible, and 3) they may not be prepared to alter their view of themselves or the universe as required by a belief in ESP. If these beliefs are changed to ones that accept ESP and clairvoyancy, then both ESP and clairvoyancy become easier. I also discovered this in my personal unpublished experiments with ESP and the conscious influence of random-event generators, both in 1993. The more I believed that I could do it, the better my results.

Wayne Dyer's book is *You'll See It When You Believe It* (William Morrow, 1989)

For a summary analysis of sheep-goat experiments, see Tony Lawrence, 'Gathering in the sheep and goats: A meta-analysis of forced choice sheep-goat ESP studies, 1947–1993', *Proceedings of the Parapsychological Association 36th Annual Conference*, M. J. Schlitz, ed., 1993, 75–86

Chapter 9: Who am I?

For a great book discussing the nature of our being see Eckhart Tolle, *The Power of Now* (New World Library, 1999)

For a description of spiritual amnesia, see Neale Donald Walsch, *Conversations with God: Book 1* (Hampton Roads, 1995)

Chapter 10: Love, Fear and Biology

The references for some of this chapter are listed in other chapters, because most of the research quoted is a summary of pieces quoted in previous chapters. For ease I have listed some of the specific sources here again.

For the effect of love on atherosclerosis in rabbits, see R. M. Nerem, M. J. Levesque and J. F. Cornhill, 'Social environment as a factor in diet-induced atherosclerosis', *Science*, 1980, 208, 1475–6

For the effects of a loving environment on the growth of the prefrontal lobes in the brains of infants and children, see Joseph Chilton Pearce, *The Biology of Transcendence* (Park Street Press, 2002)

The example of the cacti giving up their thorns when they were tenderly spoken to can be found in the book *Autobiography of a Yogi* by Paramahansa Yogananda (Self-Realization Fellowship, 1946), which is dedicated to the memory of Luther Burbank.

For studies on the effects of appreciation, care and compassion, as well as anger and frustration, on the heart and immune system, see:

- R. McCraty, M. Atkinson, W. A. Tiller, G. Rein and A. D. Watkins, 'The effects of emotions on short-term power spectrum analysis of heart rate variability', *Am. Journal of Cardiology*, 1995, 76, 1089–93

- G. Rein, M. Atkinson and R. McCraty, 'The physiological and psychological effects of compassion and anger', *J. Advancement in Med.*, 1995, 8(2), 87–105

For a summary of the effects of maternal touch on gene expression, see Ernest L. Rossi, 'Psychosocial genomics: Gene expression, neurogenesis, and human experience in mind-body medicine', *Advances*, 2002, 18(2), Winter, 22–30

For the effects of love and intention on DNA, see:

- G. Rein and R. McCraty, 'Structural changes in water and DNA associated with new physiologically measurable states', *Proc. Society for Scientific Exploration Conf.*, Austin, TX, June 1994

- G. Rein and R. McCraty, 'Local and non-local effects of coherent heart frequencies on conformational changes of DNA', *Proc. Joint USPA/IAPR Psychotronics Conf.*, Milwaukee, 1993

The above references are also cited and summarized in William A. Tiller, *Science and Human Transformation: Subtle Energies, Intentionality, and Consciousness* (Pavior, 1997)

Chapter 11: Mass Reality

For a metaphysical view of the mass creation of reality, see Jane Roberts, *The Individual and the Nature of Mass Events (A Seth Book)*, (Prentice-Hall, 1981)

For information on the Hundredth Monkey and similar experiments, see Thom Hartmann, *The Prophet's Way* (Mythical Books, 1997)

Chapter 12: DNA II

For information on string theory, see Brian Greene, *The Fabric of the Cosmos* (Allen Lane, 2004), and Stephen Hawking, *The Universe in a Nutshell* (Bantam, 2001)

Information about cyclic spurts of growth of the brain can be found in Joseph Chilton Pearce, *The Biology of Transcendence* (Park Street Press, 2002)

For information on waves of gene expression in the growth of the central nervous system, see X. Wen, S. Fuhrman, G. Michaels, D. Carr, S. Smith, J. Barker and R. Somogyi, 'Large-scale temporal gene expression mapping of central nervous system development', *Proceedings of the National Academy of Sciences*, 1998, 95, 334–9

For information about sounds and harmonics, see www.soundintentions.com

On the Higher Self choosing the genes, there is no contradiction with the laws of genetics and inheritance. I believe that each Higher Self chooses particular genes within the framework of what is possible within such laws. The Higher Self presumably chooses the parents that are most likely to produce the desired characteristics. At the root level, once characteristics are chosen by the Higher Self, the vibrations condense into particles which eventually become the DNA. At the physical, observable, level, the intention of the Higher Self presumably influences the 'random' way the genes of both parents mix to produce the unique genetic code of the foetus. Perhaps the randomness in the process of inheriting genes is not so random!

For information about man-made damage to rainforests and to biodiversity, see Thom Hartmann, *The Last Hours of Ancient Sunlight* (Mythical Books, 1998), and the section 'Earth Changes' in the appendix of *The Prophet's Way* (Mythical Books, 1997)

Chapter 13: Personal Responsibility
Chapter 14: Three Simple Rules

There are no cited references for chapters 13 and 14. However, for teachings and stories of love and kindness I would recommend the works of Gary Zukav and Wayne Dyer, PhD, as well as the *Chicken Soup* series founded by Jack Canfield and Mark Victor Hansen and the *Conversations with God* books by Neal Donald Walsch.

For an inspirational true story about love, forgiveness and personal transformation, see Immaculée Illibagiza, *Left to Tell* (Hay House, 2006)

Further Reading

The following is a list of books that I have found particularly inspirational and that have, to a degree, influenced my philosophy and understanding. It is by no means a definitive list of what to read, merely some of the books that I have personally been inspired by and that may assist you in your journey.

Spiritual, Philosophical and Self Help

Brandon Bays, *The Journey*, Thorsons, 1999

Greg Braden, *The Isaiah Effect*, Harmony Books, 2000

Jack Canfield and Mark Victor Hansen, *Chicken Soup for the Soul* (series), Health Communications Inc., 1993

Wayne Dyer, *You'll See it When You Believe It*, William Morrow, 1989

, *Getting in the Gap: Making Conscious Contact with God through Meditation*, Hay House, 2003

–, *The Power of Intention*, Hay House, 2005

–, *Inspiration: Your Ultimate Calling*, Hay House, 2006

Shakti Gawain, *Creative Visualization*, Whatever, 1978

Thom Hartmann, *The Prophet's Way*, Mythical Books, 1997

–, *The Last Hours of Ancient Sunlight*, Mythical Books, 1998

David Hawkins, *Power vs Force*, Veritas Publishing, 1995

Louise Hay, *You Can Heal Your Life*, Hay House, 1984

Esther and Jerry Hicks, *Ask and It Is Given*, Hay House, 2005

–, *The Amazing Power of Deliberate Intent*, Hay House, 2006

Dee Hock, *Birth of the Chaordic Age*, Berret-Koelher, 1999

Immaculée Ilibagiza, *Left to Tell*, Hay House, 2006

Byron Katie, *Loving What Is*, Harmony Books, 2002

Ian Pollock and Ed Bernd, *Silva Method*, Silva Method Publishing, 2001

Tony Robbins, *Awaken the Giant Within*, Summit Books, 1999

Eckhart Tolle, *The Power of Now*, New World Library, 1999

–, *Stillness Speaks*, New World Library, 2003

–, *A New Earth*, Penguin, 2005

Neale Donald Walsch, *Conversations with God* (series), Book 1: Hampton Roads, 1993

Jane Roberts, *Seth Speaks*, Prentice-Hall, 1972

–, *The Nature of Personal Reality*, Prentice-Hall, 1974

–, *The Individual and the Nature of Mass Events*, Prentice-Hall, 1981

Paramahansa Yogananda, *Autobiography of a Yogi*, Self-Realization Fellowship, 1946

Gary Zukav, *The Seat of the Soul*, Fireside, 1990

Scientifically Inclined

Jim Al-Khalili, *Quantum: A Guide for the Perplexed*, Weidenfeld & Nicholson, 2003

Will Arntz, Betsy Chasse and Mark Vicente, *What the Bleep Do We Know?* (DVD), Lord of the Wind Films, 2005

Herbert Benson, *Timeless Healing*, Simon & Schuster, 1996

Phillip Callaghan, *Paramagnetism: Rediscovering Nature's Secret Force of Growth*, Acres USA, 1995

Deepak Chopra, *Quantum Healing*, Bantam, 1989

Larry Dossey, *Healing Beyond the Body*, Shambhala, 2001

Masaru Emoto, *The Hidden Messages of Water*, Sunmante Publishing, 2001

Richard Gerber, *Vibrational Healing for the 21st Century*, Eagle Books, 2000

Malcolm Gladwell, *The Tipping Point*, Little, Brown and Co., 2000

Amit Goswami, *The Self-Aware Universe: How Consciousness Creates the Material World*, Tarcher/Putnam, 1995

Brian Greene, *The Fabric of the Cosmos*, Allen Lane, 2004

John Gribbin, *In Search of Schrödinger's Cat*, Black Swan, 1984

Stephen Hawking, *The Universe in a Nutshell*, Bantam, 2001

Dharma Singh Khalsa, *Meditation as Medicine*, Pocket Books, 2001

Bruce Lipton, *The Biology of Belief*, Mountain of Love, 2005

Lynne McTaggart, *The Field*, HarperCollins, 2001

Carolyn Miller, *Creating Miracles: Understanding the Experience of Divine Intervention*, H. J. Kramer, 1995

Joseph Chilton Pearce, *The Biology of Transcendence*, Park Street Press, 2002

Candace Pert, *Molecules of Emotion*, Scribner, 1997

Matt Ridley, *Nature via Nurture*, Fourth Estate, 2003

Ernest Rossi, *The Psychobiology of Gene Expression*, W. W. Norton & Co, 2002

Tim Spector, *Your Genes Unzipped*, Robson Books, 2003

Michael Talbot, *The Holographic Universe*, Grafton Books, 1991

William Tiller, *Science and Human Transformation*, Pavior, 1997

James Watson, *DNA: The Secret of Life*, Arrow, 2004

Gary Zukav, *The Dancing Wu Li Masters*, William Morrow, 1979

Index

About the Author

David R. Hamilton gained a first-class honours degree in chemistry, specializing in biological and medicinal chemistry, and a PhD in organic chemistry before going on to be a scientist in the pharmaceutical industry in 1995. Over the next four years he also served as an athletics coach and team manager for one of the UK's top athletics clubs. He left both roles in 1999 and has since worked as a motivational speaker, co-founded an international relief charity, co-organized a 9-day, 24-event festival of peace called Spirit Aid and worked as a college lecturer in both chemistry and ecology. He has been featured on TV and radio and been the subject of national newspaper articles. He spends most of his time writing, giving talks and leading workshops.

For additional information, including details of events, lectures and workshops, see:

www.drdavidhamilton.com

David is coming to a town or city near you!

In powerful, live, not-to-be-missed talks, David discusses how the mind affects the body and the circumstances of our lives.

For a list of towns and cities and for more information, or to sign up for David's free e-newsletter, featuring new scientific studies in mind–body science, visit
www.drdavidhamilton.com.

We hope you enjoyed this Hay House book.
If you would like to receive a free catalogue featuring additional
Hay House books and products, or if you would like information
about the Hay Foundation, please contact:

Hay House UK Ltd
Unit B • 292 Kensal Road • London W10 5BE
Tel: (44) 20 8962 1230; Fax: (44) 20 8962 1239
www.hayhouse.co.uk

****

Published and distributed in the United States of America by:
Hay House, Inc. • P.O. Box 5100 • Carlsbad, CA 92018-5100
Tel: (1) 760 431 7695 or (800) 654 5126; Fax: (1) 760 431 6948 or (800) 650 5115
www.hayhouse.com

****

Published and distributed in Australia by:
Hay House Australia Ltd • 18/36 Ralph St • Alexandria NSW 2015
Tel: (61) 2 9669 4299 • Fax: (61) 2 9669 4144
www.hayhouse.com.au

****

Published and distributed in the Republic of South Africa by:
Hay House SA (Pty) Ltd • PO Box 990 • Witkoppen 2068
Tel/Fax. (27) 11 706 6612 • orders@psdprom.co.za

****

Distributed in Canada by:
Raincoast • 9050 Shaughnessy St • Vancouver, BC V6P 6E5
Tel: (1) 604 323 7100 • Fax: (1) 604 323 2600

****

Sign up via the Hay House UK website to receive the Hay House
online newsletter and stay informed about what's going on with
your favourite authors. You'll receive bimonthly announcements
about discounts and offers, special events, product highlights,
free excerpts, giveaways, and more!

www.hayhouse.co.uk

NOTES

NOTES

NOTES

NOTES